SHIPWRECKS OF NORTH EAST SCOTLAND
1444 –1990

Also by David M Ferguson

The Wrecks of Scapa Flow
Shipwrecks of Orkney, Shetland and the Pentland Firth

SHIPWRECKS OF NORTH EAST SCOTLAND
1444–1990

DAVID M FERGUSON

ABERDEEN UNIVERSITY PRESS
Member of Maxwell Macmillan Publishing Corporation

First published 1991
Aberdeen University Press

© David M Ferguson 1991

British Library Cataloguing in Publication Data

Ferguson, David M. (David Magnus), *1939–*
Shipwrecks of North East Scotland 1444–1990
I. Title
363.12309412

ISBN 0 08 0412173

Typeset from author generated discs by
Hewer Text Composition Services
Printed by Athenaeum Press Ltd

Contents

List of illustrations

Acknowledgements

It would have been impossible to write this book without the assistance and encouragement of a large number of people. I would like to thank in particular - John McLean, Coxswain, Peterhead Lifeboat, for his hospitality and providing information on the station; Isabella Deans, Local Studies Department, Aberdeen Central Library, for locating most of the photographs in this book and the photocopying of a huge amount of research material; Judith Cripps, Archivist, Town Clerk's Department, City of Aberdeen, for her great assistance in locating records of early shipwrecks; John Edwards, Curator, Aberdeen Maritime Museum, for allowing access to unpublished material on north-east shipwrecks and providing photographs from the museums collection; Eddie Gunn, Wick, whose efforts in the preparation of the *John O'Groat Journal* index made a long difficult task infinitely easier; the anonymous newspaper indexers in Wick, Inverness, Elgin and Aberdeen whose work provided the backbone for my newspaper research; Philip Thomas of Thornliebank for sources of official returns on nineteenth century shipping casualties which once again were invaluable; Captain K. J. Douglas-Morris for explaining the Byzantine complexities of the Admiralty filing system in use during the Napoleonic Wars; Dr Peter Anderson of the Scottish Record Office for extremely useful suggestions on possible sources of information on early Scottish shipwrecks; Sutherland Manson, Thurso, for information on and photographs of Caithness shipwrecks; my brother James whose advice and assistance provided a huge amount of material which would not otherwise have been available; Commander D.T. Ancona, Chief

Coastguard, London, and J.P. Mickleburgh, Deputy Regional Controller, H.M. Coastguards, Aberdeen for access to local records without which information on some notable rescues would have been very incomplete; Paul Davis and R. Barry Cox, R.N.L.I. Headquarters, Poole, for providing research material from station records; and finally Rear Admiral G.S. Ritchie Retd, Collieston, for providing a wealth of local information.

Thanks are also due to the following persons and organisations; Peter Buchan, Peterhead; the editor of the *John O'Groat Journal*; the staff of Special Collections, King's College Library, Aberdeen; John Rainie, Inverurie; the staff of West Register House, Edinburgh; Mrs J.E. Chamberlain-Mole and Rex Findlay, North East of Scotland Museums Service, Peterhead Arbuthnot Museum; the staffs of Aberdeen Central Library and Woodside Library, Aberdeen; the Honorary Secretaries of Wick, Fraserburgh and Peterhead Lifeboats; Mr and Mrs Tom McCallum, Stromness; Information Section, Lloyds Register of Shipping, London; Wick Heritage Centre; C.H. Milsom, Editor of *Sea Breezes*; James G. Cordiner, Arbroath; Mrs A. Williams, Inverness Central Library; Wendy Ferguson, Aberdeen; Graham Hope of the *People's Journal*; the staffs of Dundee Central Library and the Mitchell Library, Glasgow; the Countess of Aberdeen, Haddo House, Aberdeenshire; Stephen Smith of the *Buchan Observer*.

Finally, thanks are due to my editor, Dr John Smith of the Centre for Scottish Studies, Aberdeen University, for his encouragement and correction of the not inconsiderable number of grammatical and spelling errors in the original manuscript. Any errors of fact are my own.

Introduction

With over 1,200 shipping casualties identified it has been possible to describe only a representative sample in this book, with some spectacular incidents having to be omitted. Having said that, the terrible storms of 1800, 1875, 1876 and 1942 have been described in detail as they give a vivid illustration of the hazards that had to be faced by the men who went down to the sea in ships.

For sailing vessels, a lower size limit of 50 tons register has in general been used. As a rough rule of thumb this has meant that the lower limit by rig has included sloops but excluded smacks. However, the loss of the *Thames*, a smack of substantial size which featured in a particularly spectacular incident, has been included. For steamships and motor vessels a lower limit of 100tons gross has been used.

Location of wrecks has proved a problem, some positions given in early accounts being vague in the extreme, for example, "on the Buchan coast". Problems also arise during both world wars, severe censorship limiting most accounts of marine and war losses to official records which have proved in some cases to be less than accurate. With some casualties several different locations exist for where they were sunk and depend on which source is consulted. As an example the Swedish steamer *Fram* was torpedoed to the west of Fraserburgh on 1 February 1940 and four positions for her loss are available, namely, from the Hydrographic Department, German U-boat records, Lloyds Loss Books and H.M. Coastguard.

It would be totally unfair to blame the crews of sinking ships for this inaccuracy; their main aim was to get off as quickly as possible before they went down with their stricken ships with little enough time to send off an SOS and a hastily estimated position. The *Fram* is perhaps an extreme example but readers should understand that while every effort has been made to locate vessels accurately their true position may differ substantially from that given in contemporary records. Because of the sheer number of casualties on the section of coast between the River Don and Belhelvie locations of wrecks shown in the 'chartlet' are only approximate. Likewise positions have only been indicated generally where there are heavy concentrations of casualties, for example, off Aberdeen and Rattray Head

As reports of casualties occurring on the Caithness and Sutherland coasts prior to 1836 are virtually non-existent there has been an unavoidable bias in favour of other areas up to that time. Dates given are those quoted in contemporary sources and with early casualties there may be discrepancies with the present day calendar where the original source has made no distinction between Old and New Style calendars.

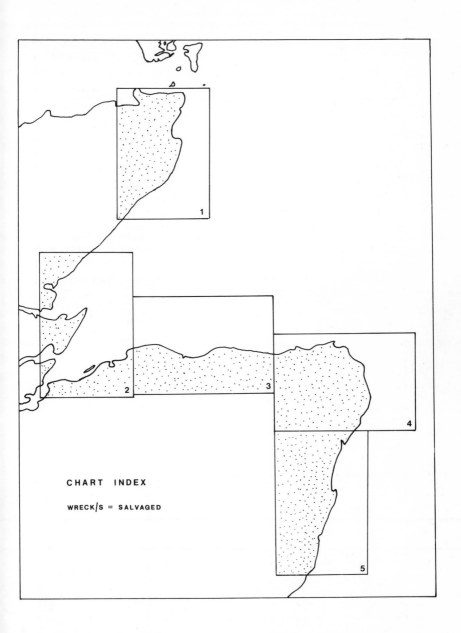

CHART INDEX

WRECK/S = SALVAGED

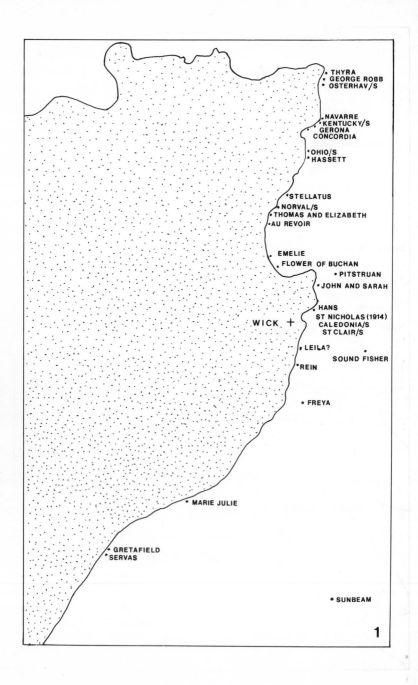

THYRA
GEORGE ROBB
OSTERHAV/S

NAVARRE
KENTUCKY/S
GERONA
CONCORDIA

OHIO/S
HASSETT

STELLATUS
NORVAL/S
THOMAS AND ELIZABETH
AU REVOIR

EMELIE
FLOWER OF BUCHAN
PITSTRUAN
JOHN AND SARAH

HANS
ST NICHOLAS (1914)
CALEDONIA/S
ST CLAIR/S

WICK +

LEILA?
SOUND FISHER
REIN

FREYA

MARIE JULIE

GRETAFIELD
SERVAS

SUNBEAM

1

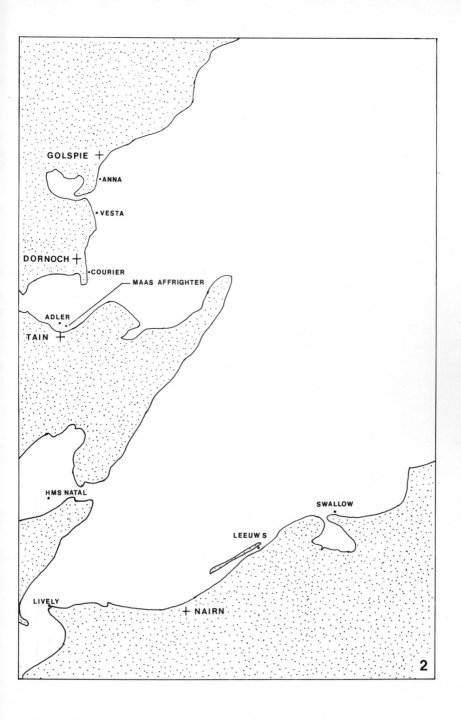

GOLSPIE

•ANNA

•VESTA

DORNOCH

•COURIER

MAAS AFFRIGHTER

ADLER

TAIN

HMS NATAL

SWALLOW

LEEUW S

LIVELY

NAIRN

2

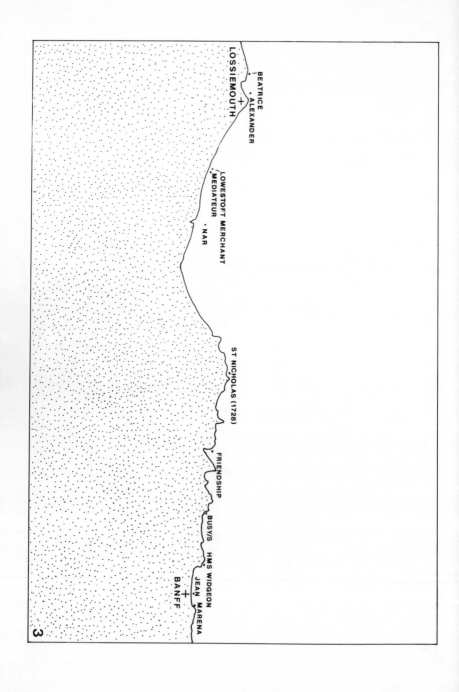

LOSSIEMOUTH
BEATRICE
ALEXANDER

LOWESTOFT MERCHANT
MEDIATEUR
NAR

ST NICHOLAS (1728)

FRIENDSHIP

BUSY/S
HMS WIDGEON
JEAN MARENA
BANFF

3

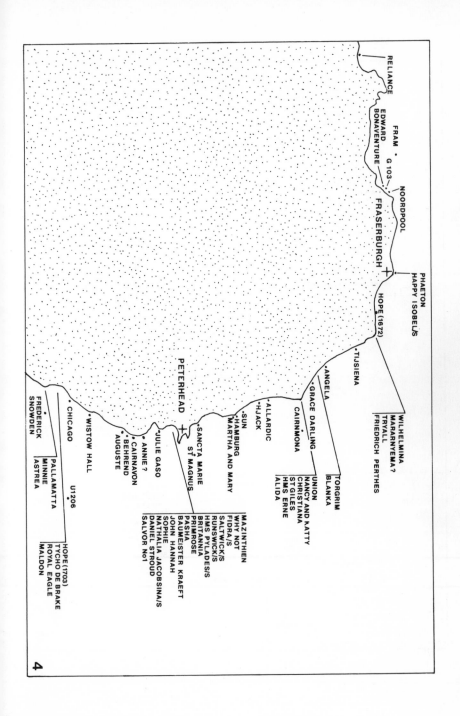

RELIANCE

EDWARD BONAVENTURE

FRAM   G 103

NOORDPOOL

FRASERBURGH

PHAETON
HAPPY ISOBEL/S

WILHELMINA
MARARNYEMA?
TRYALL
FRIEDRICH PERTHES

HOPE (1672)

TIJSIENA

ANGELA

TORGRIM
BLANKA

GRACE DARLING

PETERHEAD

CAIRNMONA

UNION
NANCY AND KATTY
CHRISTIANA
ST GILES
HMS ERNE
ALIDA

ALLARDIC

H.JACK

SUN

HAMBURG
MARTHA AND MARY

CHICAGO

WISTOW HALL

SANCTA MARIE
ST MAGNUS

JULIE GASO

ANNIE ?

CAIRNAVON

BEHREND

AUGUSTE

MAZINTHIEN
WHY NOT
FIDRA/S
SALTWICK/S
RUNSWICK/S
HMS PYLADES/S
BRITANNIA
PRIMROSE
PASHA
BAUMEISTER KRAEFT
JOHN HANNAH
SOPHIE
NATHALIA JACOBSINA/S
DANIEL STROUD
SALVOR No1

FREDERICK
SNOWDEN

U1206

PALLAMATTA
MINNIE
ASTREA

HOPE (1703)
TYCHO DE BRAKE
ROYAL EAGLE
MALDON

4

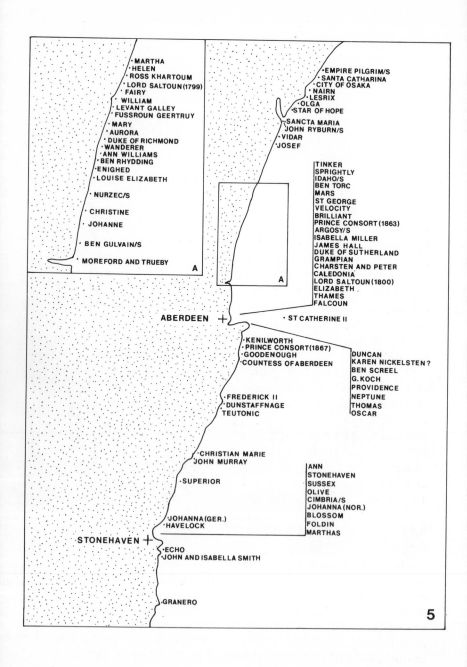

MARTHA
HELEN
ROSS KHARTOUM
LORD SALTOUN (1799)
FAIRY
WILLIAM
LEVANT GALLEY
FUSSROUN GEERTRUY
MARY
AURORA
DUKE OF RICHMOND
WANDERER
ANN WILLIAMS
BEN RHYDDING
ENIGHED
LOUISE ELIZABETH

NURZEC/S

CHRISTINE

JOHANNE

BEN GULVAIN/S

MOREFORD AND TRUEBY

EMPIRE PILGRIM/S
SANTA CATHARINA
CITY OF OSAKA
NAIRN
LESRIX
OLGA
STAR OF HOPE
SANCTA MARIA
JOHN RYBURN/S
VIDAR
JOSEF

TINKER
SPRIGHTLY
IDAHO/S
BEN TORC
MARS
ST GEORGE
VELOCITY
BRILLIANT
PRINCE CONSORT (1863)
ARGOSY/S
ISABELLA MILLER
JAMES HALL
DUKE OF SUTHERLAND
GRAMPIAN
CHARSTEN AND PETER
CALEDONIA
LORD SALTOUN (1800)
ELIZABETH
THAMES
FALCOUN

A

A

ABERDEEN +

ST CATHERINE II

KENILWORTH
PRINCE CONSORT (1867)
GOODENOUGH
COUNTESS OF ABERDEEN

DUNCAN
KAREN NICKELSTEN?
BEN SCREEL
G. KOCH
PROVIDENCE
NEPTUNE
THOMAS
OSCAR

FREDERICK II
DUNSTAFFNAGE
TEUTONIC

CHRISTIAN MARIE
JOHN MURRAY

SUPERIOR

ANN
STONEHAVEN
SUSSEX
OLIVE
CIMBRIA/S
JOHANNA (NOR.)
BLOSSOM
FOLDIN
MARTHAS

JOHANNA (GER.)
HAVELOCK

STONEHAVEN +

ECHO
JOHN AND ISABELLA SMITH

GRANERO

5

The North East of Scotland

For the purposes of this book the coast of North East Scotland has been taken as extending from Duncansby Head in the north to Tod Head in the south. The coast is a combination of wild rugged cliffs interspersed with long sandy shores. Flagstones or sandstones provide the foundations of the slablike cliffs of Caithness, schists the Sutors of Cromarty, while the rugged coasts of Banffshire, Aberdeenshire and Kincardine are composed for the most part of ancient metamorphic rocks and granites.

It was recognised from earliest times that the extreme north-east coast of Aberdeenshire was a severe hazard to shipping. In fact, about one-third of all the shipping casualties in the area covered in this book occurred on the twenty-five miles of coast between Fraserburgh and Cruden Bay. For this reason the first lighthouse was established at Kinnairds Head in 1787. This was converted from Tower Castle and was lit only eleven months after the establishment of the Northern Lighthouse Board. Thereafter, lighthouses had to be built from scratch. The next one, at Buchan Ness, was lit in 1827 with a full series of coastal lights being established during the remainder of the nineteenth century.

Prior to the nineteenth century the rescue of crews was attempted entirely on the initiative of local inhabitants. These were frequently undertaken in truly appalling conditions and would, all too frequently, end in disaster with the rescue boat swamped or wrecked and all on board lost. Lifeboats were progressively stationed round the coast in the nineteenth century, the earliest being established at Aberdeen in 1802 and the last station opened at Cromarty in 1911. A particular feature of early rescues was the willingness of all sections of the local population, not just those connected with the sea, to man rescue boats. At Wick a local watchmaker was frequently noted as turning out with the lifeboat while at Fraserburgh a shoemaker was gallantly involved in an early rescue.

Other early rescue equipment included Captain Manby's Patent Apparatus which was basically a small cannon ball with a line attached, fired from a mortar. One account of an early rescue noted with satisfaction that the cannonball had landed in the casualty's cabin. One is left wondering whether the sailors on this particular case were in more danger of being brained than of drowning. Later line-throwing equipment used rockets which were less lethal and more accurate . Helicopters now undertake a considerable number of maritime rescues but have not completely supplanted the lifeboat or rocket apparatus.

Early mariners had little in the way of navigational aids which nowadays are taken for granted. Lighthouses and coastal beacons were nonexistent, while on board the mariner had the use of sandglasses, logboards, cross staffs, dry compasses and leadline to help him shape his course. Although not a chart, Lindsay's *A Rutter of the Scottish Seas* published about 1540, gave a reasonably comprehensive description of the principal 'Hauens, Sandis and Daungeris' of the north-east coast together with relevant sailing directions. A century and a half later Captain Grenville Collins produced his magnificent *Great Britain's Coasting Pilot* which included charts of the coast and principal ports of North East Scotland. Present-day Hydrographic Department charts are based on survey work going as far back as 1834.

Apart from Duncansby Head, where spring tidal rates of over ten knots have been reported running just west of the Pentland Skerries, the remainder of the coast has much more modest tidal strengths with a maximum of three knots off Buchan Ness and one knot off Girdle Ness. In the days before radar, another hazard was haar or coastal fog which occurred principally in summer months when south-easterly winds were cooled over the North Sea. This was caused by a relatively stable weather system and the coasts of North East Scotland could be shrouded for days in thick fog which reduced visibility to virtually nil. These same south-easterly winds blowing for days at a time in winter could produce terrifying storms such as those of January 1800 and November/December 1876 which resulted in catastrophic shipping losses.

Of all of the anchorages on the coast that of the Cromarty Firth is by far the best with it being described in Lindsay's *Rutter* as the finest in the 'yle of Britain' [for all] '...kynds of wyndis and storme'. It was used as a major fleet base by the Royal Navy in two world wars and is now an important centre for the repair and maintenance of drilling platforms. Aberdeen, the main port for north-east Scotland, is of great antiquity and was known to Ptolemy in the second century AD by the name *Devana* 'the town of the two waters'(Rivers Dee and Don). Little is known of its earliest history but by the twelfth century trade links with the Continent were well established with exports of hides, salmon, wool and furs. In spite of periodic set-backs due to war, piracy and pestilence the port gradually increased in importance and from being little more than a tidal creek it had become, by the end of the nineteenth century, a major centre for fishing and shipbuilding. Today, Aberdeen is the main oil supply base for the North Sea, the fishing and shipbuilding industries having been in decline since the end of the Second World War.

Peterhead, another oil supply base and fishing port, has a large Harbour of Refuge built by convict labour in the late nineteenth century, which gives excellent protection to shipping against easterly winds. Elsewhere, the coast is dotted with small ports and fishing villages which swarmed with shipping during the nineteenth century but are now deserted or only used by yachtsmen. It is difficult to realise now that up to the end of the nineteenth century ports like Banff and Wick had direct and energetic trading links with the Continent and the rest of mainland Britain, exporting fish, wool and grain in exchange for timber, iron, flax, hemp and merchant goods. For towns like these, improved inland communications with the rest of Britain resulted in the apparent contradiction of a major narrowing of their coastwise and continental trading links as goods could be exported and imported more cheaply through the larger ports which were now accessible by land. In the case of Wick, major contributory factors were the collapse of the herring industry, more or less coinciding with the loss of East European markets after the First World War. Other 'ports', some little more than a slot in some towering cliff, like Whaligoe in Caithness reached by a flight of 350 flagstone steps, closed with the exhaustion of inshore fishing stocks.

There are three areas along the coast where shipping losses tend to be concentrated, namely in the vicinity of the ports of Aberdeen and Wick and at the extreme north-east corner of Aberdeenshire. In the case of the ports, casualties were mainly due to vessels lying off or trying to enter being driven ashore by stress of weather. With the twenty-five miles of coast between Fraserburgh and Cruden Bay there were two main types of loss, those sunk offshore in wartime due to enemy action and those which went ashore in heavy weather. During both world wars, shipping, either independently routed or in convoy, had, for operational reasons, to pass relatively close inshore of Buchan Ness. This concentration of shipping proved a tempting target for enemy units which caused serious losses to Allied and neutral merchant fleets in both wars. Those ships lost on the coast were almost exclusively sailing vessels driving before south-easterly gales being unable to weather the extreme north-east corner of Aberdeenshire. Of the twelve hundred or so casualties which are known to have gone ashore between Duncansby Head and Tod Head one-third occurred between Fraserburgh and Cruden Bay.

Earliest Times

Prior to the eighteenth century information on shipwrecks in north-east Scotland is virtually nonexistent. The early burgh records of Aberdeen contain a brief reference to an un-named 'barge' that was 'brak' in the vicinity of the town in the late summer of 1444. Apparently the crew and supercargo had no 'playnt' to make against the inhabitants of the burgh. On the contrary, 'the gude men of the town had done right weel to them'.

Unfortunately such behaviour was very much the exception, the crews and owners of wrecked ships having all too good grounds to complain about the behaviour of the 'country people'. This was certainly true in the case of the *Edward Bonaventure*, bound from the White Sea to London with the Russian Ambassador and his entourage, which was wrecked in Pitsligo Bay west of Fraserburgh on 10 November 1556. Under the command of Richard Chancellor, the great Elizabethan navigator, she had sailed on 20 July in the company of three other English vessels with a cargo of furs, wax, yarns, and other goods to the huge value of £20,000 sterling. Apart from this the Ambassador carried gifts for Queen Mary from the Emperor of Russia which included, 'six timbers of sables rich in colour and hue', 'thirty Lusannes(?) large and beautiful' and 'a large and fair white Jerfawcon' (hawk). Severe weather was encountered in the North Sea and the *Edward Bonaventure* was separated from the other vessels. A landfall was made on the coast and the ship anchored in Pitsligo Bay just west of Rosehearty with a severe northerly gale blowing.

In the continuing gale the *Edward Bonaventure* 'being beaten from her ground tackles was driven on the rocks ashore where she was broke and split in pieces'. 'The Grand Pilot', that is Chancellor, tried to reach shore in one of the ship's boats with the Russian Ambassador and seven of his retinue but it was overwhelmed in the surf. Chancellor, the seven Russians and most of the seamen manning the boat were drowned, the Ambassador only being saved with great difficulty. In fact, of the one hundred or so people on the wrecked ship practically none reached the shore alive. Worse still, as Hakluyt describes in his *Discovery of Muscovy* the goods and cargo washed ashore were 'by the rude and ravenous people of the Country thereunto adjoining, rifled, spoyled and carried away...'.

The incident caused acute embarrassment to the governments of both Scotland and England who dispatched commissioners to the scene to try to recover the stolen property. They met with little enough success only 'divers small parcels of wax and other trifling things' being handed over by the 'poorer sort of Scottes'. A large number of the local inhabitants were summoned to Edinburgh 'to account for their stewardship' but this appears to have been ignored as there is no record of any of the culprits being tried or convicted. The unfortunate Russian Ambassador remained in the district till the following February before continuing overland to London.

A rather convoluted case brought before the Scottish Privy Council involved the *Falcoun* of Norway wrecked at Aberdeen in July 1584. She had been bought in Norway on credit along with the cargo (unstated) by two of the shiftier inhabitants of Leith. Having taken possession, they set sail but were by 'contrare windis drevin in the firth of Aberdeen'. While the two new owners were ashore 'doing of sundrie thair necessar effears' the crew 'falling at stryff and debait amomgis themselffis' the 'said ship was brokin and maid unable to mak saill'. The ship and cargo were promptly sold 'to mak penny thairof' and the two rogues disappeared with the proceeds. Two years later they were still being pursued through the courts by the original owners for the purchase price of '400 gude auld Dutch dollars'.

One of the most intriguing wreck sites on the north-east coast is to be found at St Catherine's Dub just north of Collieston which is supposed to be named after an Armada galleon wrecked there in 1588. Although a great deal has been written about it there is very little hard evidence and the casualty is something of an enigma. That a wreck exists there can be no doubt; from 1840 onwards a series of diving expeditions on the site have yielded a number of cannon, an anchor and a quantity of ships' fittings. A Lieutenant Patterson of the local coastguards raised two cannon in the early 1840s while another, recovered in 1855 by the Rev James Rust minister of Slains, was presented to the Earl of Aberdeen and still lies in the grounds of Haddo House. In May 1876 a further two cannon and an anchor were brought to the surface during a dive organised by the Countess of Erroll and presented to Queen Victoria. Finally, in the summers of 1970 and 1971 two small cannon, some chain fittings and a large iron anchor were raised. The anchor has been preserved and is on display outside the Arbuthnot Museum in Peterhead.

There is no contemporary evidence which could identify the wreck; two *Santa Catalinas* (with slightly differing spellings) sailed with the Armada but are known to have returned to Spain. The political uproar which the arrival of the Spanish fleet caused in both Scotland and England led to greatly increased intelligence activity and the wreck of one of the vessels from that fleet on the Scottish coast would have been reported to the authorities in either Edinburgh or London. In fact the relevant calendars of state papers make no mention of such an event. There is a possibility that the vessel was wrecked while bringing Spanish arms and ammunition to aid the Earl of Erroll's rebellion some time between 1588 and 1594 when Slains Castle was destroyed by James VI.

With almost continuous hostilities between England and France the early years of the seventeenth century were wild and dangerous times. The coasts around the British Isles swarmed with privateers, in reality legalised pirates, who preyed on merchant shipping. Late in 1627, or early the following year, the *Sanct Marie* of Lubeck on a voyage from Spain with a cargo of wine, sugar and 'pokes' (parcels) of aniseed was taken by a Scottish privateer. The prize crew tried to sail her to Leith but were by 'distresse of weather in a tempestous storme' driven ashore just north of Peterhead. In a letter to the Privy Council in Edinburgh from Inverugie Castle, dated 20 January 1628, the Countess Marischal gave details of the wreck. The 'countrie people that are not answerable to his Majesteis lawes' had ransacked the ship, and what remained had been spoiled by salt water and also there was 'much leikage of wynes'. In the absence of her husband, who claimed rights of Admiralty for that stretch of coast, this formidable woman had salvaged what was left of the cargo, transported it to drying lofts to save as much as possible and made an inventory of the goods recovered. The tone of the letter is self-confident and businesslike as befits a woman married to the Earl Marischal (this gentleman, one of the more ferocious members of the Scottish aristocracy, was much given to besieging towns whose inhabitants were, in the Earl's opinion, of insufficent or incorrect religious zeal. Aberdeen was to receive his attentions in the following decade with disastrous consequences for that town). The Privy Council replied firmly but deferentially (it would have been most unwise to have offended the Countess and hence her husband), requesting that the ship and salvaged cargo be handed over to two commissioners appointed by the Council. At the time the royal finances were much straitened with 'grite burdynis lyand thairupon' and the Council made an order for any proceeds from the sale of the cargo of the *Sanct Marie* to be paid to captains of three of the king's ships for 'wadgeis addebit'.

As has been said these were wild and dangerous times in Scotland and the early letter books of Aberdeen Town Council vividly describe the exactions of lawless armies, pestilence, famine and losses at sea. In the decade between 1639 and 1648 the ship owners of Aberdeen sustained losses due to piracy and shipwreck to the tune of some half a million pounds Scots. Even allowing for the fact that there were only twenty pounds Scots to one pound sterling and the figures were probably an early exercise in creative accounting (they had been prepared in 1648 for an enquiry into the ruinous state of the town's finances and almost certainly inflated), it is clear that the town had suffered a series of major calamities at sea. The losses included five ships wrecked on the north-east coast. Details are unfortunately sparse but the vessels ranged from 'ane great fleboat' loaded with deals, tar, butter and tallow cast away in the Moray Firth and valued at £10,000 Scots to 'ane bark of Aberdeen quhairof Still, Master loadit with lime cast away in Aberdeen sands', valued at £1,333. 6s 8d Scots. Some, like Captain Still's vessel, were probably only a few tens of ton burden whereas the one commanded by a William Scott wrecked in the entrance to Aberdeen harbour and loaded with timber was a substantial ship of 140 tons.

Shipwrecks have always been regarded as a more or less legitimate target by those living on the coast. When the *Hope* of Leith was totally wrecked on the Sands of Cairnbulg in November 1672 the local inhabitants descended on it like a swarm of locusts and carried off everything they could lay their hands on. The authorities in Aberdeen and a local landowner, Alexander Fletcher the Master of Saltoun, whose tenants had been heavily involved in the plundering, decided to prosecute as many of the wreckers as possible. Over forty of them were brought before a series of specially convened courts and while most confessed to having taken some minor piece of wreck the proceedings were notable for what was not admitted. Andrew Massie in Phingask rather daringly confessed to have received a brass compass, two or three ells of 'small towis' (rope) and some iron nails from two boys but most of the finds seemed hardly worth the trouble. John McBeth in Pitblae (just south of Fraserburgh) only 'found' an old plaid and pair of breeches on the sands while Robert Anderson from Newmill on the Water of Philorth picked up an old hair stuff coat which he offered to a Mr Jossie ' but (he) refused samen being of no value'. Why John Cruden appeared before the court is something of a mystery as he helped bury fourteen bodies 'being my Lord Saltounis command' and denied stealing anything. However, the court records are incomplete and it is not known what happened to those who were convicted.

By the end of the seventeenth century the British colonies in America provided cargoes of tobacco, sugar and timber for returning ships with rich rewards for those returning safely. The *Ann* of Newcastle was not one of them; having sailed from Maryland with a cargo of tobacco on 20 August 1693, she arrived off Stonehaven at the beginning of October and had to anchor in the bay due to contrary winds. With the weather deteriorating a pilot was embarked but almost immediately the bower anchor cable parted and with 'the wind blowing extremely the ship was forced on the shore and did bulge'. The *Ann* was refloated with great difficulty and then run ashore again by the master 'for preservation of their lives'. Most of her cargo and part of the hull were washed away and the remains, 'altogether damnified' sold for £200 to cover expenses.

There being little ready money in circulation in seventeenth century Scotland payment of such items as taxation and rentals in the remoter parts of the country were made in kind. In two cases this proved to be a case of putting all of one's eggs in a basket that got wrecked. In October 1677 a ship carrying all the rents in kind from Orkney and Shetland for the whole of the previous year and part of 1675 was wrecked at Fraserburgh 'where the ship, goods and men, one boy excepted, were wholly lost'. Exactly twenty years later, in the autumn of 1697, the *Elizabeth* of Kirkwall having sailed from Shetland with a cargo of rental goods in the form of butter, oil and calf skins was driven northwards for three days by contrary winds having lost her mast and sail. The wind then swung to the north and a jury sail was rigged during which time from 'the want of provisions perished five or six which was thrown overboard'. Finally, having reached Aberdeen the *Elizabeth* struck on the bar while being towed into harbour and went to pieces. Some of the cargo was carried upriver as far as the Bridge of Dee (over two and a half miles) with the remainder being ' scattered up and down (the coast) in a hundred places'. The cargo that was salvaged was in such poor condition that it was given away to 'the country people'.

When an unnamed ship bound for Aberdeen with a cargo which included wool, candles, brandy and hats. was driven ashore on the south side of the Ythan estuary in October 1703 the temptation proved too great for the people in the surrounding district and large quantities of the cargo and remains of the ship were carried off. The Provost and Baillies of Aberdeen learned of the affair and having rights of Admiralty over that section of coast dispatched an official to the scene to investigate the thefts and summon any malefactors to appear before a specially convened court. From the list of wreck goods recovered most of those living in the area appear to have been involved, from Mr William Gordon, schoolmaster, to the widow Christie and her son. It emerged at the court proceedings that apart from stealing from the wreck the inhabitants were busy stealing from each other as well. Thus Robert Findlay admitted under oath that he had gathered some wool in a 'pock' (bundle) which was promptly stolen when he laid it down. Robert Bein's son was somewhat luckier; having salvaged some candles he sold them to a Major Buchan for 18s Scots. All in all people seem to have been carried away by the affair; it is a little difficult to imagine what William Gordon the schoolmaster could have done with an anchor and mast which he admitted to stealing. Those who confessed or were found guilty were fined £50 Scots each and ordered to hand over everything they had stolen.

Contemporary accounts of early casualties are often written in language which today sounds archaic and quaint. The sale of the wreck and cargo of the *Hope* of Northburg (Nordborg in Jutland) in 1707 is an excellent example and comes from the Propinquity Books in Aberdeen City Archives.

'7 March 1707. In presence of Baillie Ross and Strachan.

The said day compeared [appeared] Hary Elphinston and Andrew Jaffray, Merchants in Aberdeen, and being solemnly sworn deponed that the ship called the Hope of Northburg being a hoy [a single masted vessel usually rigged as a sloop] in the Kindom of Denmark being stranded and disastered in the Bay of Cruden upon the sands near by the Slaynes [Old Slains Castle] that they bought the said ship as she was disastered from Jesper Yuirisone Merchant in Sunderburg [Sonderburg in Jutland] for seventy dollars [probably Danish rixdollars]. As also they bought the wholl cargo of Herring being eighteen lasts and a halfe [about thirty seven tons] for four pund Scots money each barrell of the said herring, and also that they bought thirty ston wooll at five pounds Scots money each ston. . . . and this is the truth as they shall answer to god.

On 16 January 1708 two Dutch vessels the *Levant Galley* of Amsterdam and the dogger *Fussroun Geertruy* drove ashore in a storm at Belhelvie about six miles north of Aberdeen. Details of the circumstances surrounding their loss are vague but in the case of the former (also called the *Smyrna Galley*) most of the crew reached the shore alive and a substantial part of the cargo was salvaged. The dogger, bound for Madiera and Curacao, went to pieces with the loss of her crew and cargo which was 'sanded and drove to sea'. For Aberdeen the wreck of the galley proved a major windfall as the cargo, which included spices, logwood, cloth and books, was purchased by some merchants and handed over to the city's magistrates for the benefit of the community.

The salvage of the wreck and her cargo was a huge operation which lasted over six months. Almost everyone benefited one way or another, none more so than the keeper of a nearby inn who sold a stupendous amount of food and drink. Literally hundreds of receipts for ale, wine, punch, tobacco, pipes, victuals, writing paper, pens, ink and candles survive in the Aberdeen city archives. For example, one of the Provost's bills for drink, candles and horse hire for *nine days* in February came to £251. 19s 10d Scots. Thomas Simm, cooper, claimed £13 Scots for making nine herring barrels to hold salvaged spice while four shillings drink money was given to some seamen employed on salvage operations to make them work harder. Another receipt, dated 10 March 1708, reads 'To George Leiper a poorman in footie [Footdee in Aberdeen] Six Shillings Scots Money for his finding, saving and bringing of some hebrew books to the Magistrates this day'. With such a valuable wreck the Magistrates wisely posted an armed guard of two officers and eighteen men who were issued with shot and powder to the tune of £1. 9s 6d Scots. Some of the timber salvaged from the two wrecks was transported to Aberdeen and used to re-floor the harbour weigh house and strengthen the head of the south pier.

'With hundreds of the rabill stealling'

At times the authorities were quite unable to maintain any
semblance of order at the scene of shipwrecks with the 'mobb'
completely gaining the upper hand. In the middle of November
1716 the *Duncan* of London, Charles Norman master, had sailed
from 'Ferimus' on the Moray Firth (not positively identified but
possibly one of the 'Ferrys' on the western shore of the Firth)
bound for London with a valuable cargo of 'effects' belonging to
the Earl of Sutherland and a Sir William Gordon. The vessel,
described as a galley (in fact, she was probably rigged as a ship
or three-masted barque), had set sail in light winds which had
fallen calm before veering to the east and rising to storm force
when the ship was off Girdle Ness. In spite of this the captain
carried a full press of canvas until the crew, fearing the ship
would drive under, persuaded him to shorten sail. In the rapidly
worsening conditions the *Duncan* was slowly driven towards the
land with the foresail splitting, the chain plate and ruff tree
breaking and one of the crew being washed overboard and lost.

By this time the ship was close inshore off the rocks of Girdle
Ness with the storm showing no signs of abating. The master
wanted to cut down the masts so that the ship would ride more
easily, and then anchor off but the crew would not agree and
'cryed out for the Lord's sake to put her on shore if possible to
save ther lives'. There was little alternative for the unfortunate
Captain Norman but to put the ship's helm over and allow her
to drive ashore on the rocks a little after highwater. As it was
before dawn and pitch dark a gun was fired as a distress signal
and a light displayed. This attracted the 'country people' and
with the ship now high and dry the supercargo managed to

scramble ashore where he unsucessfully tried to persuade them
to help and unload the ship. A kedge anchor was set out but
because of the 'rabill' only a few items were brought ashore
before the master and supercargo 'took horse' for Aberdeen to
seek help from the magistrates.

When they returned to Girdle Ness two hours later with some
of the town officials and a party of soldiers the ship had gone to
pieces and the shore was 'lyned with hundreds of the rabill
stealling and running away with all that came on shore'. As soon
as anything was saved it was taken to a tent set up on the shore
as a store from which it was promptly stolen by the mob in spite
of being fired on by a detachment of local troops who were
standing guard. By this time the magistrates and town officers
had also arrived on the scene and they 'threatned, beat and
whypt the rabill' in a hopeless attempt to maintain order. In the
end, and on the advice of the magistrates, all salvage operations
were abandoned and Captain Norman sent everything that had
been saved into Aberdeen with 'a great pairt lost in that
passage'.As a result of the incident proceedings were brought by
the Provost and Baillies against a list of over one hundred
persons who were accused of stealing from the wreck of the
Duncan. Unfortunately no record of the trial or verdicts and
sentences survives.

Apart from the activities of the 'rabill' the authorities also had
to deal with the occasional rogue. A favourite swindle was to
scuttle some grossly over-valued old vessel, claim the money for
it and a fictitious cargo and disappear with the proceeds before
the insurers got wind of the fraud. With such slow and uncertain
communications in the early eighteenth century it could be
months before the swindle came to light. This was obviously
what Captain Thurren Stocksen had in mind when he insured
the *Sancta Maria* of Bergen and her supposed cargo of tar and
deals on a voyage from Norway to Britain for a large sum on the
Amsterdam market. In early June 1722 some white fishers from
Newburgh came across the vessel lying at anchor off the mouth
of the River Ythan. With the weather being 'fair and easy' there
would have been no difficulty in bringing her into the estuary.
She was still lying there when the white fishers put to sea early
the following morning to shoot their lines. Shortly afterwards
and without warning the *Sancta Maria* fell over on her port side.

When the boats managed to row alongside they found that she was a small 'croayer' of about fifty tons burden with no one aboard.The two anchors at which she had been riding were weighed and the ship, still afloat but lying on her beam ends, was towed towards the Ythan estuary. As it was half flood there was insufficient water on the bar and the mainyard fouled on the bottom about half a cable from the entrance.

Almost simultaneously Captain Stocksen arrived on the scene in a boat from Collieston, a small fishing village just up the coast from Newburgh. Apart from asking the white fishers whether they had weighed the anchors or cut the cables he seemed surprisingly uninterested in salvaging his ship or her cargo. In view of the master's lack of interest the fishers put off to sea again with the intention of hauling their lines and then returning to the *Sancta Maria* to try and tow her into the Ythan. By the time they returned all the running and standing rigging had been stripped by the captain and the ship had started to break up. The captain was still on the scene and took charge of the two anchors and cables offering the fishermen anything that they could salvage from the wreck. He then rowed off in the direction of Collieston and took no further part in the proceedings. Once the ship had broken up it became obvious that the 'cargo' was virtually non-existent and only consisted of a small parcel of spars, there being no sign of any deals or tar. It was not until the following October that the authorities in Aberdeen, at the request of the insurers in Amsterdam, started enquiries into the circumstances surrounding the loss of the *Sancta Maria* by which time Captain Stocksen had long since disappeared.

Some idea of the strength of easterly gales and the effect they had on shipping in the North Sea is well illustrated by the circumstances surrounding the loss of the *Sun* of Lubeck at St Fergus on 17 January 1728. She had sailed from her home port bound for Bordeaux on 4 December and did not clear the Naze in Norway until over a month later due to contrary winds. When off the Dogger Bank the wind rose to storm force south-south-east with the *Sun* unable to carry anything but her mainsail and driving before the storm. By the time Buchan Ness was sighted and the ship some three hundred miles off course, the 'cookroom' had been washed away and the crew were too exhausted from having to continually man the pumps to go aloft and secure a foresail brace when it broke loose. When Peterhead came in sight the master who was manning the helm with the cook bore away to the north in a vain attempt to weather Rattray Head. By now the pumps were unable to cope and with the water gaining rapidly he had little choice but to put his helm over and allow the *Sun* to drive onto the relative safety of the Sands of St Fergus before she sank under her exhausted crew.

Three days later with the storm having swung northerly the *St Nicholas* of Stockholm was wrecked at Portknockie with heavy loss of life. She had been on a voyage from Amsterdam to Stockholm with an extremely valuable cargo which included tobacco, wine, silk stuffs, figs, tea, coffee and pepper. As the master was amongst those lost the supercargo, Peter Tirnman, as the most senior surviving member of the crew, made urgent application to the local Admiral Substitute William Lorimer of Dytach, for assistance in protecting the wreck and cargo from further damage by the sea and, more importantly, the attentions of the 'country people'. Lorimer immediately issued instructions that anyone who found wreck goods at 'the coast side' and surrendered them within three days would receive one-fifth of their value. Those who did otherwise would be prosecuted 'to the outmost extent of the law and [so] that none may pretend ignorance' this was to be 'intimate publickly from the Latron of Every Parish Church'. Unfortunately some of the inhabitants of the nearby town of Cullen must have been extremely deaf or not in the habit of going to church as a mob from there stole everything they could get their hands on 'and offered Violence to the poor distracted Gentleman passenger aboard'. Worse still, noted the scandalised Admiral Substitute in a letter to the Magistrates of Cullen, some of the outrages had taken place on the sabbath. He was a great deal less than diplomatic and lectured them at length on their duty as magistrates of the 'Burrow', the shortcomings of the inhabitants and the need to uphold the rule of law. Not unnaturally the magistrates took violent umbrage at the letter and replied huffily that 'upon our narrow enquiry [we] cant discover any Such unacountable practices'. Furthermore they had 'by touk of drum prohibited any of our Inhabitants from Stealing or Imbazling the wrack of the Said Ship'.

It is clear that in spite of the authorities' best efforts, they faced an uphill task and a great deal was stolen from the wreck.

An undated Memorandum survives listing the principal offenders and their booty. Two skippers had managed to salvage the wrecked ship's rudder and sold parts of it to various people, one of whom included the Reverend Kerr, minister of the nearby church of Rathven! All of the seamen of 'Broadhyth of ffindochtie' and the very oddly named Rotten Sloach (apparently part of present-day Portessie) were implicated in the theft of tobacco, pipe staves, barrel bottoms and writing paper. Isobel Murray had sold some pipe staves to James Michie, a cooper in Cullen who had carried them off 'under silence of night'. Finally John Mair, a seaman in Portknockie, had managed to slip ashore with some coils of rope stolen from the wreck and buried them in his midden. In the end what was left of the wreck and cargo were sold by public auction and by the time expenses had been deducted the net total remaining was only £386 Scots. Perhaps one should not think too ill of the local inhabitants as amongst the list of expenses is the item 'To the men who went to the rock and saved the sailors £6'.

By the eighteenth century the herring fishing industry in northern Scotland was sufficently well organised for ships to run cargoes from there to the rest of Britain on a regular basis. In the case of Caithness, vessels anchored off the coast and the herring in barrels was brought out to them in small boats. It was an extremely precarious business as most of the coast was backed by high flagstone cliffs with the harbours, such as they were, lying at the head of little creeks. Mention has been made in the introduction of Whaligoe with its 350 steps; Staxigoe just north of Wick was another such port although a great deal easier of access. At the end of October 1730 the London registered sloop *John and Sarah* had anchored off the latter to take on a cargo of herring. In a sudden storm she drove from her anchors and grounded on the rocky shore at Staxigoe. In a salvage operation lasting a month directed by the ship's master, Andrew Cummins, the cargo was unloaded and the ballast jettisoned to lighten the ship. With the assistance of local fishermen suitably fortified with ale (cost fifteen shillings) she was refloated at the end of November and towed to Wick. In spite of laying out three shillings on tallow and nails to repair the worst of the leaks Captain Cummins had to hire a party of men 'pumping all they were able to doe' to keep the sloop afloat while it was under tow. For his efforts the captain was paid the rather miserly sum of two shillings and six pence *per diem*.

Apart from herring, the coasts of the Northern and Western Isles yielded a considerable tonnage of kelp every year. This was produced by burning dried seaweed gathered from the shore,the resulting ashes being shipped to England for use in the manufacture of glass and chemicals. The *Tryall* of Aberdeen, James Thomson master, had sailed from North Uist in the middle of October 1742 laden with sixty-seven tons 'Amsterdam weight' of kelp bound for Rawcliffe on the Humber. Having had to put into Stromness due to adverse winds, she lay wind bound for several days before resuming her voyage. Shortly after midnight on 22 November 'the darkness of the night not giving the opportunity of plainly discovering the land' the ship struck on the rocks of Cairnbulg Briggs just east of Fraserburgh. With the helm broken, their ship holed and pounding badly in the heavy surf the crew had little choice but to abandon ship in their small boat only getting ashore with great difficulty. At low water the master and crew went back out to their ship to discover that it was full of water and the cargo of kelp 'damnified'. A few days later, with some of the cargo salvaged the ship broke up completely and the remainder was washed away. In a sworn statement made before one of the baillies in Aberdeen Captain Thomson blamed his misfortune on an 'indraught of the flood-tide which haled the ship more in towards the land than calculation'. In plain English the unfortunate captain had misjudged the strength of the tide.

Although only a sloop, the *Happy Isobel* of Fraserburgh which stranded off her home port on 19 November 1750 was notable for the quite extraordinary amount of correspondence which she generated. The Vice-Admiral Depute who dealt with the casualty, one Alexander Ritchie, was a chronic letter writer who expended a huge quantity of paper and ink in saying very little beyond trivialities and complaints. All his unfortunate correspondents must have uttered a groan (this writer certainly did) as they ploughed their way through his interminable ramblings about the wreck. The *Happy Isobel* had sailed from Rotterdam the previous month with a general cargo of grain, wool, flax, hemp, writing paper, pan brass, spirits and garden tools which the master hoped to run ashore in North East Scotland as contraband. She put into Cromarty possibly due to stress of weather, and sailed from there with Thomas Forbes the local tidesman (customs official) still on board. Having been fed some cock and bull story about sailing for Bergen, the unfortunate official was unceremoniously dumped ashore at Peterhead. The sloop was next reported to have briefly anchored in Fraserburgh Bay on 15 November before weighing and standing off to the southward. Four days later she again anchored in the bay but ran onto rocks close to the harbour entrance while running for shelter in a freshening wind. The customs officers pounced and insisted that once unloaded the cargo should be securely lodged under the joint custody of themselves and local admiralty court officials.

In fact the court officials seized the salvaged cargo and could only be persuaded to release it in the following March. Some of it was sold the following month but a considerable quantity of damaged goods which were unsaleable remained in a 'garrot'. For the next ten years they were the subject of an interminable correspondence between Alexander Ritchie and Aberdeen Town Council who were admirals of the coast. Ritchie was a complainer on an heroic scale; nobody turned up for one of the sales, some of the owners of goods would not come and take them away, the owner of the 'garrot' was dunning him for unpaid rent, some of the remaining goods were completely ruined, in March 1752 he was still storing a double hogshead of spoiled hemp and some rusty garden tools (along with other items) and finally, no one would pay his accounts. It was only after ten years that the flow of letters mercifully ceased and for all the writer knows the goods are still mouldering away in some 'garrot' in Fraserburgh.

The authorities continued to experience problems with the 'mobb' when the snow *Martha and Mary* of North Berwick went ashore on Scotstown Head during the night of 6 February 1760. On this very exposed part of the coast she soon broke up and the lighter cargo of bales of flax and hemp were washed ashore and buried in the sand while the balance, consisting of iron bars remained on the bottom. As usual the wreck attracted a mob 'who came and forcibly digged up' the cargo and 'in the most daring and audacious manner threatened, abused and insulted the guard'. Worse still, on the following day about fifty men arrived and when the guard tried to stop them from removing cargo they were tied up with ropes, dragged up and down the beach and threats made to throw them in the sea. The ringleaders were immediately arrested by admiralty court officials and turned out to be a pretty sorry crew as they included an old woman and a half-wit. Those convicted were fined, but as Robert Garden, local Admiral Substitute (showing considerable humanity and understanding) later remarked in a letter, they were quite unable to pay being more or less destitute and hoped that part of the fines would be remitted. In an operation lasting two months most of the iron was salvaged, there being an added incentive. Garden noted with approval (the Scots' reputation for being canny is not wholly undeserved), 'As there is not one bar of iron in Peterhead the whole might be sold at a good price'. He showed more of his understanding in a letter to the Aberdeen Town Clerk who was unwise enough to query some of the labour charges. 'If they will please consider the boisterous weather the guards had and the uncommonly severe work in hauling out and up the cargo they won't think the wages so extravagant'.

It is difficult to know what to write about the wreck of the *Annie* at Boddam in 1772 as she may not have even existed. There exists in the folklore of the northeast of Scotland the following malicious little poem;

> The *Annie* it cam' roun' the Coast
> And a' the hands on it were lost
> Except the monkey that climbed the post
> And the Boddamers hanged the monkey O!

This rather barbaric act was supposed to have been due to a decision made in 1674 by the Scottish Court of Session. It decided that if any living thing survived on board a vessel cast ashore it could not be considered a wreck (in that case all of the crew had been lost and an ox was the sole survivor). Having hung the wretched animal the Boddamers, just to hedge their bets, supposedly gave the remains a full Christian burial before ransacking the wreck. At least that is one of the versions that the writer remembers hearing as a young child. As a similar poem about Hartlepool also exists readers will have to make up their own minds about the wreck of the *Annie*. Whatever really happened the folk of Boddam are still known to this day as 'Monkey-hangers', although not usually to their faces.

To give some idea of the scale of smuggling in North East Scotland during the eighteenth century no less than thirteen vessels engaged in the trade are known to have been stranded while 'hovering' off the coast between 1728 and 1786. In one incident two ships, both laden with contraband tea, went ashore on the night of 3/4 November 1786, the *Jean* of Findhorn on Banff Bar, and the *Friendship* of Portsoy on the beach at Sandend. The position of William Aven, one of the Tidesmen in Portsoy became decidedly precarious when it was discovered that his son was one of the crew of the *Friendship* and that he had failed to call out any of the other customs officials on learning of the wreck. Aven claimed to have been roused from his bed at three o'clock in the morning by a commotion outside his house and was told about the wreck by a woman he did not recognise. He said he was so concerned that he rushed straight off to the scene of the wreck without informing any of his colleagues and found that his son and some of the crew had reached shore safely. About half an hour afterwards the ship broke up completely and huge amounts of tea in boxes, casks and canisters came ashore but Aven made no proper attempt to secure it or call for assistance. It was not till later that morning that the other Tidesman in Portsoy learned of the wreck and took immediate steps to seize what remained of the cargo and lodge it securely. In fact over three and a half tons of tea, most of it soaking and useless, was recovered, with the near certainty that the 'country people' had managed to 'run' most of the undamaged cargo. Aven came in for bitter criticism for his handling of the affair but does not seem to have suffered any disciplinary action.

In September 1796 the *Earl of Derby* bound for Liverpool with a cargo of deals and iron from St Petersburg ran ashore in Fraserburgh Bay. Only about half of the cargo was salvaged before the ship went to pieces and the lower section of the hull sank in the sand. As iron carried a particularly high rate of duty and to guard against any loss to the revenue the customs authorities had no less than five officials superintending salvage operations. Faced with having to bear such exorbitant costs the owners decided to cut their losses and sold ship and cargo where they lay. A Mr James Reid having recovered part of the cargo eventually submitted his account of charges to the Collector of Customs in Aberdeen. In all they totalled the then astronomical sum of over £1,100 Sterling and included such strange and wonderful items as, '9 spades, "A high price" £2. 5s 3d', '4 Ankers of Whisky [over thirty gallons!] Expended in Drams £16' and two years hire of horse and boy £72. It is not clear whether they were ever paid. Finally, in the summer of 1807 most of the sand was washed away from the wreck and it was possible for her to be dragged closer inshore. About forty tons of iron were salvaged and advertised for sale in the *Aberdeen Journal*, if not exactly treasure from the deep then an unexpected bonus.

4

The Great Storm of 1800

The new century began with a series of appalling storms which blew more or less continually during the first three weeks of January. Contemporary accounts are vague with reports from Caithness and Sutherland virtually non-existent but it is known with reasonable certainty that at least thirty vessels were driven ashore during the period. In the south-easterly gales which were accompanied by sleet and snow there was no shelter on the Aberdeenshire coast and ships were forced to run for the relative safety of the Moray Firth. Five vessels were driven ashore on the first day of the storm, which actually started on the last day of the old century. North of Aberdeen, the master of the *Martha* of Aberdeen was the only man that survived when his ship, together with the Fraserburgh brigantine *Lord Saltoun* and the *Neptune* of Aberdeen, all went to pieces on the sands of Belhelvie. Further south at Stonehaven the brigantine *Stonehaven* and the *Sussex* of Aberdeen also went ashore, fortunately without loss of life.

There was a lull on New Year's Day before seven more ships were driven ashore with heavy loss of life on 3 January; two unidentified vessels at Portlethen, two Sunderland registered brigs at Aberdeen and a brig and two sloops at Collieston. Another four ships were stranded on the following day but because of the total disruption to communications caused by the storms, two which had occurred in the extreme north of Scotland were not reported in the Aberdeen papers until the following month. There was another temporary improvement in the weather until 7 January when another storm sprang up and eleven more ships were driven ashore and completely wrecked,

almost all of them on the coast between Aberdeen and Rattray
Head.

Little is known about most of them except the Swedish brig
Phaeton bound from Cayenne to Gothenburg which came
ashore near Fraserburgh. Three of her crew and three
passengers, a French priest and a mother and child, were
drowned with the remaining crew and four other French
passengers being saved, ('...these passengers were possessed of
plenty of gold and other valuables...' noted the *Aberdeen Journal*
with a true Aberdonian's interest in such matters). Although a
state of war existed between Britain and France at that time the
Foreign Secretary directed that the surviving passengers should
be found berths on the first available ship sailing to a neutral
port on the Continent. (In those more easy-going times when
nations went to war hostilities were regarded to some extent as a
private arrangement between opposing armies and navies,
civilians being able to come and go more or less as they
pleased, an eminently sensible arrangement that Bonaparte was
in the process of destroying.)

Later in the same month on 21 January the brig *Lord Saltoun*
and sloop *Peggy and Mary* were driven ashore on Aberdeen
beach 'in the midst of the most severe storm of wind and snow'.
Lord Seafield who commanded the local barracks 'exerted
himself in an uncommon manner', directing rescue operations so
successfully that both crews were safely brought ashore. His
lordship was also pleased to distribute £10 amongst the rescuers.
Apparently in the same storm – contemporary accounts are
infuriatingly vague – the *Britannia* bound for Aberdeen with a
cargo of bark went ashore at Peterhead while running for
shelter, with only her master and a boy being saved.

During the next two years there were mercifully few shipping
casualties around the northeast coast. One of the most
interesting was the 1,100 ton Danzig ship *Tycho de Brake*
which had the dubious distinction of being wrecked twice. She
had first gone ashore on Sanday in the Orkneys on 27 September
1801 while on a voyage from Danzig to Liverpool with a cargo
of timber and wheat. After an initial salvage operation she had
been beached on Stronsay and then purchased by the Aberdeen
firm of Fraser and Mole. The ship had been refloated after a
false bottom had been constructed during the winter but sadly

when almost at her destination, she went ashore at Cruden Bay
on 24 August 1802 with the loss of one man. Unfortunately little
else is known about this remarkable salvage operation, which
given the size of the ship and severe technical difficulties, was an
extraordinary achievement.

The year 1803 opened with a series of south-easterly gales
which inevitably caused shipping casualties around the coast and
a huge amount of wreckage came ashore on the beach at
Cairnbulg on 8 January. It consisted of the lower section of a
ship's hull, masts and rigging, together with a feather bed,
printed silk handkerchiefs and a considerable quantity of
oranges. There was no sign of the crew and at first it was
thought that the vessel was a Dutch or Danish Indiaman. Word
about the rich pickings soon reached the ears of the local
population who made off with everything they could get their
hands on. With the wholesale looting the local Justices of the
Peace ordered a strict search of all houses and buildings in the
vicinity. A cart-load of plundered goods was seized and the
ship's register also came to light which identified her as the
Russian galliot *Mararnyema*. Over the next few days five bodies
were washed ashore, and one wearing a shirt with large silver
buttons and having a gold ring on one finger was presumed to be
that of the captain.

Despite an unfortunate habit of making off with any wreck
goods that came ashore those living on the coast frequently went
to extraordinary lengths to rescue survivors. In the spring of
1803 after a severe gale the inhabitants of the little Banffshire
fishing village of Gardenstown awoke to find that a large
amount of wreckage had been washed ashore during the night of
19 April. A search of the coast revealed the remains of a ship in
Whale Cove at the bottom of cliffs on the west side of Gamrie
Bay. A lone survivor was spotted clinging to a rock a little way
offshore where he had spent the night. It was only at low water
that some of the young men from the village managed to
clamber down the towering cliffs, scramble over the rocks and
haul the exhausted and frozen man back up to safety. The
wrecked vessel proved to be the *Reliance* of Newcastle, 198 tons
register, which had sailed a few days previously from Shields
bound for Jamaica with a cargo of coal. Colin Burn, the sole
survivor, described as a native of Montrose, had signed on the

day before the ship had sailed and was only able to identify one of the six bodies that came ashore. From the report in the *Aberdeen Journal* 'by an intelligent Correspondent in Gardenstown' it appears that the master was running too close inshore while trying to shelter under the lee of the land.

At the end of 1803 the north-east was again struck by a hurricane and several ships and a number of fishing craft were lost between Stonehaven and Kinnairds Head. A remarkable feature was the number of large well found vessels which were lost during the storm. The Shields brig *Thomas*, coal laden, struck on the rocks at Nigg saltworks just south of Aberdeen on 19 December. Her master and six crew members were washed away and drowned when the main-mast on which they had been sheltering went over the side. The Marquis of Huntly on hearing of the wreck rode to the scene 'and though the weather was inclement, continued there for some hours, appointing a guard, giving instructions, ordering spirits for those assisting, and encouraging the people to exertion.' In the event four survivors were brought alive and provided with relief by his lordship who 'humanely enquired concerning the circumstances of the men saved'.

During that night, the 1,200 ton full-rigged ship *Christiana* of Christiana (Oslo), in ballast from London for Norway, struck on the beach at Rattray Head having been blown off the Norwegian coast when in sight of her home port. In the massive surf there was no hope of any boat being launched from the shore to take off any survivors and those who had assembled on the beach were helpless spectators. Soon after daybreak two of the crew were drowned when they tried to get ashore in a boat which was immediately swamped. A third man lashed himself into another boat and after a hair raising trip through the surf was rescued from certain death by some of the large crowd of spectators who dashed into the waves and dragged him ashore. On the stranded ship some of the crew had cut down the masts in the hope that she would not break up but she finally went to pieces just as dusk was falling. Incredibly a section of the quarter deck carrying the master and eighteen of the crew was safely washed up on the beach.

Three days later on 22 December the Swedish ship *Nancy and Katty* with a cargo of salt from St Ubes in Portugal stranded on the easternmost point of Rattray Head.Through the efforts of a Mr Geddes, a farmer on the nearby Broadlands estate, who had played a major part in the rescue of the crew of the *Christiana*, all of those on board were brought off safely. The ship was completely wrecked and her cargo of salt washed away. On the following day the *Mary* of London, completely water-logged and lying on her side, stranded at Blackdog on Belhelvie Sands. She had sailed in convoy from Elsinore on 12 December with a cargo of timber from Memel and shipped so much water in the storm that she fell over on her beam-ends. Four of her men were washed overboard and drowned, two died of exposure while the remainder survived by eating two of the ship's cats!

It was almost certainly during this storm that the third rate warship HMS *York* foundered with the loss of her complement of 491 officers and men. She had been last seen on 26 December and nothing more was heard of her until wreckage started coming ashore between Cruden Bay and St Combs in the following February. Her sinking was confirmed in the middle of March when a gun carriage marked *York* together with a man's hand and a pair of officers pantaloons trimmed with red morrocco leather were found on the shore at Rattray Head. From the distribution of the wreckage it would appear that the 1,433 ton warship had sunk off Kinnairds Head. Her loss is by far the worst shipping disaster involving loss of life that has occurred off the coast of North East Scotland.

Naval losses continued, fortunately without loss of life, when the small schooner HMS *Widgeon* ran onto rocks off Blackpots, west of Banff, early on the morning of 20 April 1808. Under the command of Lieutenant George Elliot she had been ordered to proceed to Banff and advise shipping there that a convoy lying off Kinnairds Head was ready to proceed to North America. As the weather was appalling, south-east gales with snow, he decided to lie off till day break and then send a boat ashore. Before turning in for the night Lieutenant Elliot left strict instructions with the pilot and midshipman of the watch that the schooner was to be kept at least four miles off the coast during the night. At half past two the following morning the lieutenant was rudely awakened by the schooner running ashore. When he got on deck, clad only in shirt and drawers, he discovered that the pilot was below and only a boatswain's mate in charge of the watch. A gun was fired as a distress signal and although ammunition was jettisoned, water casks started, pumps rigged and a kedge anchor laid out the *Widgeon* filled within ten minutes. When it became obvious that she would become a total loss efforts were concentrated on getting everything moveable ashore. As commanding officer, Lieutenant Elliot was automatically court-martialled but completely exonerated, the loss of the schooner being 'attributed, wholly to the inattention and negligence of the Pilot, in not having put the orders he received from the Commander into execution'. He was sentenced to six months imprisonment in the Marshalsea Prison with stoppage of pay. In spite of the fact that press censorship in those days was virtually non-existent no mention of the schooner's loss appeared in any of the local papers and the details of her stranding are taken from the court-martial proceedings.

As a result of the tragic losses in 1803 a Mr Harvey of Broadlands (apparently the original name for Rattray House), whose estate was situated on the coast adjacent to Rattray Head, proposed through the columns of the Aberdeen newspapers that a subscription should be opened for the purchase of two lifeboats, to be stationed at Fraserburgh and Peterhead respectively. It was not until 15 October 1808 that the first lifeboat, stationed at Fraserburgh, entered service and rescued the crew of the Rosehearty sloop *Isabella* which had run ashore in a northerly gale in Fraserburgh Bay. The former's crew which included a shoemaker, a flax-dresser and blacksmith were unable to reach the sloop as huge waves kept driving them to leeward and they finally had to give up through sheer exhaustion. In a further attempt the lifeboat was dragged well up-wind of the stranded sloop before being launched with a fresh crew of volunteers from the beach. This time they were able to row sufficiently far off shore to keep clear of the worst of the surf and succeeded in taking off the *Isabella*'s crew 'to the inexpressible joy of those present'.

In the early nineteenth century with no statutory survey regulations governing ships or their crews some vessels put to sea in a lamentable condition. When the galliot *Wilhelmina* of Helsingfors bound from Gothenburg to Liverpool with a cargo of tar and deals encountered a gale off the north of Scotland at the end of November 1808 she literally came adrift at the seams. Shortly after springing a leak her deck separated from the hull with the former breaking into several sections which the crew managed to lash together with stout warps. In this precarious state and only floating on her cargo the galliot drifted onto the rocks of Cairnbulg Point early in the morning of 1 December. As the weather remained moderate a local yawl was able to take off the entire crew but not surprisingly she soon broke up and by the following month wreckage and barrels of tar were coming ashore as far south as Arbroath.

During the Napoleonic Wars the seas around the British Isles swarmed with enemy privateers whose activities were only partly checked by the Royal Navy. On 31 December 1808 the Danish schooner *Goodenough* with a cargo of timber was captured in the North Sea by the Swedish privateer *Moreland* and a prize crew put aboard to sail her to Sweden. The schooner was soon overtaken by an easterly gale and the prizemaster's son lost overboard. In the continuing gale the schooner was unable to beat off the Scottish coast and drove ashore below the cliffs at Cove on 7 January. When she struck the prize master was thrown off the bows and drowned while trying to conn the schooner into a small creek. As there was no way in which anyone on land could board the stranded vessel the three remaining survivors were hauled up the cliffs on ropes.

In order to deter privateers the Royal Navy deployed a variety of small warships such as armed cutters, schooners and sloops around the coast. Apart from their protection work they were also frequently called upon to assist merchant vessels disabled by stress of weather, any salvage money being a very welcome bonus for officers and men. Thus on 4 November 1811 the sloops of war HMS *Fly* and HMS *Pylades* towed two disabled ships into Peterhead harbour with the latter also having on board the crew of a water-logged Danzig vessel. After landing the survivors the *Pylades* anchored off and her commander, Captain George Ferguson, went ashore to visit his father at Pitfour House. Early the following morning, with Captain Ferguson still ashore, the sloop's anchor chain parted in a sudden squall and she grounded on the Horseback Rock close to the harbour entrance before any sails could be set. After a hurried return from Pitfour House, Captain Ferguson, assisted by a large number of the inhabitants

of Peterhead succeeded in refloating the sloop by throwing all
the guns overboard and cutting away her mast. Captain
Ferguson, in an attempt to clear his name, asked that he be
court-martialled but this was declined by the Admiralty. He was
retired on half-pay in 1815 at the end of the war with France,
eventually being promoted an admiral in 1861 through the
process of dead men's shoes.

The same squall also drove the brigantine *Primrose* onto rocks
nearby. As she had fallen on her beam-ends the crew were able
to scramble ashore along the masts. Next day, the shroud
lanyards were cut and the brigantine righted herself when the
masts went by the board. Sadly, while she was being hauled into
the harbour a rope gave way, striking her master on the head
killing him instantly.

At this time Aberdeen was a major whaling port and in spite
of the war the trade continued with some of the vessels being
armed with carriage guns to protect them against enemy
shipping. On 1 April 1813 after a spell of unseasonably fine
weather five Aberdeen whalers were riding at anchor in the bay,
prior to departing for the Davis Straits, when the weather
abruptly deteriorated. Two of them, the *St Andrew* and the
Oscar weighed and tried to stand out to sea to clear Girdle Ness
when the wind fell light and both were carried close inshore by
the tide. Being unable to maintain way in the light airs they had
no choice but to anchor off in a very perilous situation.
Disastrously, the wind abruptly strengthened, rapidly rising to a
full north-east gale with snow and both whalers started to drag
towards the shore. The *St Andrew*, lying slightly further out to
sea, cut both cables and getting under way with stay and mizzen
sails set just managed to weather Girdle Ness. Tragically the
Oscar was too close in shore to have any chance of clearing the
land and she was driven onto the rocks of Greyhope Bay where
she almost immediately started to break up. Both masts quickly
went by the board and two of her boats filled with men who had
managed to get away from the wrecked whaler were soon
swamped in the surf. Although lying close to the shore there was
no way in which the huge crowd of onlookers could offer any
assistance because of the massive surf. The forecastle was the last
section of the hull to remain above water and five men and her
master, Captain Innes, found a brief refuge there before they

1 The whaler *Oscar* ashore at Greyhope Bay, Aberdeen, on 1 April 1813, a watercolour by an unknown artist (Aberdeen City Arts Department, Art Gallery and Museums).

were washed off and disappeared from sight. Of her complement of forty-four men, only the mate and a seaman reached the shore alive through the surging debris and surf.

There were a further series of disasters off the harbour at the beginning of 1815 when four vessels were lost trying to enter the port in an easterly gale. Shortly after midday on 26 January the brig *Caledonia*, coal-laden, foundered in the approaches with the loss of all hands after being struck by a huge sea. Then the schooner *Providence* having missed the entrance, probably due to the southerly set of the flood tide, ran ashore in Nigg Bay. Her master, the sole survivor from the crew of four, was washed ashore clinging to the main-boom. About two hours later the trading smack *Thames* on passage from London with a valuable cargo of merchant goods, two passengers and a crew of nine was flung on her beam ends at the harbour mouth. Although she righted herself she had been rendered completely unmanageable and drifted ashore among the rocks of Greyhope Bay close to where the *Oscar* had stranded. Some of the survivors took to the rigging but were soon washed off, the last two men shaking hands shortly before they disappeared, and no one reached the shore alive.

The gale continued to blow until the following weekend when on 29 January another smack by good luck and superb seamanship managed to run the gauntlet and entered the port safely. A Danish galliot, the *Charsten and Peter*, following close behind was less fortunate and having been struck on the beam by a large wave, yawed violently, grounding on the North Pier. One of her crew who jumped overboard onto rocks at the root of the pier was killed instantly when the galliot rolled on top of him. Her master and three seamen were pulled ashore by spectators on the shore and a fifth man who had also jumped overboard was picked up completely exhausted in the navigation channel by a pilot boat.

With the cessation of hostilities between Britain and France in 1815 there was a dramatic decrease in the number and size of shipping casualties around the north-east coast. Losses were, for the most part, confined to smaller coastal vessels, the number of which was also reduced by the effects of an economic slump which coincided with the end of the war. One of the larger casualties was the Aberdeen brig *Norval* on her maiden voyage to Quebec with a general cargo which was caught by the flood tide off Stroma on the evening of 5 April 1818. With the tide running at between eight and nine knots the brig was swept back out of the Pentland Firth into the North Sea. At midnight while attempting to re-enter the firth in a strong north-east wind with snow (evidently it was a late spring!) she ran ashore on Tang Head in Sinclair's Bay her master having completely underestimated the strength of the tide off Duncansby Head. Although she filled completely the *Aberdeen Journal* Shipping List reported that she was refloated the following week with the loss of her keel and stern post.

The loss of the sloop *Marthas* of Limekilns on 7 October 1822 was a particularly hair-raising incident where the unfortunate crew faced the disagreeable choice of death by drowning or incineration. She had sailed from Sunderland with a cargo of lime for Findhorn and having encountered heavy weather sprang a leak off Berwick. As is well known, when quicklime comes in contact with water it slakes and huge amounts of heat are generated. The sloop soon caught fire with the crew unable to abandon ship in the heavy seas. She was allowed to run before the wind finally driving ashore at Stonehaven with the sails spent and the vessel on fire from stem to stern. Two boats were dragged over the rocks to where the *Marthas* was lying and in spite of the heavy seas took off the sloop's crew with one of the rescuers being washed out of his boat but managing to swim ashore. Shortly afterwards the sloop was enveloped in flames and the mast fell over the side.

5

'In the most dextrous and seamanlike manner'

Although off the main shipping routes and used mainly by coastal vessels and traffic from the Caledonian Canal the extreme western end of the Moray Firth has been the scene of several spectacular wrecks. There are numerous banks and shallows between Nairn and Inverness formed from the huge amounts of sediment brought down by the River Findhorn and coastal lights were completely lacking until 1830 when a lighthouse was established at Tarbat Ness. At the beginning of 1827 northern Scotland was struck by what the *Inverness Journal* called 'a smart storm'. Early on the morning of 2 January the *Lively* of Inverness (probably a smack or sloop) bound from Wick for her home port with a cargo of merchant goods and barrels of herring struck the Riff Bank, lost steerage way and was driven, with both anchors dragging, onto the beach immediately below Fort George.

The stranded ship was seen at daybreak by Lieutenant Lindsay of the Preventative Service, who together with his own men and some of the officers and men from the 78th Regiment garrisoned at the fort succeeded in rescuing the crew and two passengers. It is clear from the *Journal's* somewhat incomplete report that at some time during the rescue things went badly wrong as it goes on to say, 'We are informed, that but for the generous exertions and self devotion of those gentlemen [from the fort], Lieut. Lindsay and his men would have fallen a sacrifice to their humane efforts'. Once on shore the survivors were taken to the fort and entertained by the officers. Some of the cargo was salvaged but later that afternoon the *Lively* broke up 'with an awful crash' with the remains of her stern being buried in the sands beside the fort. By an interesting coincidence the same issue of the *Inverness Journal* contained the report of a public meeting held at Golspie for the purpose of petitioning the Commissioners for Northern Lights about the desirability of establishing a lighthouse in the Moray Firth. The correspondence columns in that issue also carried a closely argued letter from 'A Naval Officer' about the suitability of Tarbat Ness as the site for such a lighthouse.

Those wishing to travel in North East Scotland during the first half of the nineteenth century had two choices, to either go overland by roads which were at best indifferent or sail around the coast which was usually quicker but carried the slight risk of shipwreck. Joseph Mitchell the pioneering civil engineer who built or designed many of the early roads and railways in the area gives vivid descriptions in his memoirs of travelling in those coasting vessels. Before the advent of steam they were usually smacks (of up to 200 tons burden) or latterly schooners, and called at a myriad of little ports and creeks around the coast. It was this shipping that suffered most severely in any prolonged easterly storm. In January 1830 there were appalling shipping losses along the east coast of Great Britain when it was struck by a prolonged and severe easterly gale. Although the most serious casualties occurred off north-east England at least two vessels were lost in the vicinity of Aberdeen.

The *Aberdeen Journal* reported that apart from a brief lull the storm had lasted more or less continuously for the first three weeks of January producing terrible seas on the north-east coast. The smack *Fame* of Findhorn was the first casualty when she was unable to weather the coast and grounded on the sands at Blackdog about six miles north of Aberdeen early on the morning of 21 January. She was seen at daybreak by coastguards at Belhelvie and Donmouth who immediately set off for the casualty and were able to retrieve a line veered ashore on a cask. Using a coble two of the smack's crew brought five passengers ashore and then tried to return to take off the remaining crew. Tragically, the warp parted and the two men drowned when the coble broached-to and capsized in the surf. The coastguards fired a line to the *Fame* using a Manby mortar and the nine men still aboard were brought ashore uninjured apart from the mate whose ankle had been broken when the smack struck. Once all the survivors had been taken off they and their rescuers were given much appreciated shelter at the nearby farm of Blackdog, Mr Craighead the farmer being praised for his 'benevolent exertions'. Although badly pounded by the heavy surf the smack did not break up and her cargo of merchant goods from London, badly damaged by water, was offloaded when the weather moderated for onward shipment to Inverness.

By the following morning the storm had veered to the south and the port of Aberdeen reopened. Although several vessels steered successfully through the tremendous seas after the tide flag had been raised the brig *Grampian* was thrown bodily onto the base of the North Pier having been steered too far to leeward. At the critical moment of opening the entrance the master had had to haul up into the wind and the brig fell down on the pier with insufficent room to clear it. She almost at once started to break up and with no thought for their own safety a group of spectators seized her fore-top-mast and rigging when it fell onto the pier beside them. In a frantic scramble using lifelines and any loose ropes that came to hand the master and three men were dragged to safety but one seaman and the mate, who had been stunned by the collapse of the galley, were washed away and drowned. With huge waves sweeping the pier one of the rescuers was washed off to be saved on the point of sinking through complete exhaustion by the crew of a pilot boat.

Although there could be serious loss of life involved with the wrecks of larger ships those suffered by the fishing communities were at times quite disastrous. Working a few miles off the coast in small undecked yawls their crews stood little or no chance with the sudden onset of an onshore storm. Over twenty fishermen perished on 18 November 1835 when the coast was struck by a brief but particularly severe northerly gale which only lasted for about two hours. It blew up without warning during the morning when the fishing fleets were at sea and by the time it subsided later in the afternoon boats had been driven ashore at Rattray Head, Gardenstown and Cullen. Although four larger vessels also went ashore there was no loss of life and two were later refloated. One of the most interesting and luckiest casualties was the Newcastle sloop *Busy* which had been overtaken by the storm in the Moray Firth while bound for Wick with a cargo of tallow and hemp from Leith. Her master had been forced to run before the wind and the sloop was in considerable danger of driving onto the rocks between Portsoy and Whitehills when she was seen by a shepherd. Having been a sailor in his youth he was able to signal to the crew to steer for the Burnmouth of Boyne being the only haven on that stretch of coast that offered any chance of safety. With immense good luck the *Busy* drove right into the burn grounding without damage to the ship or cargo. Her very relieved and no doubt extremely surprised captain handsomely rewarded the shepherd for his quick thinking and the sloop was towed out of the burn mouth a few days later and sailed round to Portsoy.

Occasionally the coast would be struck by storms in summer, doubly dangerous being totally unexpected. In the latter part of August 1837 a north-east gale sprang up without warning and several ships were driven ashore between Lossiemouth and Cullen. At Speymouth the sloop *Beatrice* of Leith, John Winchester master, had been lying off with a cargo of coal and iron when the wind increased during the night of the twenty-fifth to a gale. Her captain was forced to bear away for the Cromarty Firth to seek shelter but had great difficulty in preventing the sloop from falling off to leeward.The tiller broke in the heavy following sea and by now completely unmanageable she struck on the rocks off Stotfield Head. Apart from the crew of two men and a boy the captain's wife and eight year old daughter were also on board and had been locked in the cabin for their own saftey just before the sloop struck. Their cries became so heart-rending however, that Captain Winchester in tragically mistaken kindness brought them back on deck and they were almost immediately washed overboard along with the rest of the crew. The captain became entangled in some of the rigging and was washed back on board by a succeeding wave but everyone else was swept away and drowned. By now completely derelict, the sloop drifted from rock to rock before finally grounding on the Halliman Skerries. On the shore spectators could make out the lone figure of the captain standing on the deck of the wrecked sloop frantically waving for assistance. With no boats to hand a salmon coble was dragged along the shore from Lossiemouth by some workmen and put off manned by the local Lloyds agent, four shipmasters and a coastguard. They succeeded in pulling alongside the *Beatrice* where the unfortunate captain, by now suffering severely from exposure, was lowered by a rope into the boat and safely brought ashore. The sloop, launched only six months previously at Speymouth, became a total loss and was sold where she lay.

Although the first steamer had entered Aberdeen in July 1820 the wooden paddle ship *Brilliant* was the first to be lost on the coast of North East Scotland when she went ashore in the harbour entrance on 12 December 1839. At 159 tons gross she was small by present day standards but has considerable historical interest having been built at Greenock in 1821, with Bell undertaking his pioneering work on the *Comet* only nine years previously. She had sailed from Leith the previous afternoon and been overtaken by a south-easterly gale during the night. Next morning off Girdle Ness her master, Captain Wade, standing on the quarter-deck by the binnacle was thrown overboard when the ship rolled in a particularly heavy sea. (Early steamships did not have bridges as such, the wheel and engine-room controls being located on an open and unprotected section of deck. In the case of the *Brilliant* it consisted of a raised platform carried between her two paddle boxes. It was therefore not unknown for helmsmen and watch-officers of such vessels to be lost overboard in heavy weather.) As it was well before dawn there was not the slightest chance of the unfortunate man being saved and those on deck had no choice but to run for the harbour entrance.

In the beam seas the steamer was carried too far to leeward and struck the south side of the North Pier just inside the seaward end. There was considerable confusion and panic as succeeding seas drove her further onto the root of the pier with the chief engineer abandoning the engine-room and rushing on deck. The unfortunate passengers were left more or less to their own devices in the pitch darkness with the accompanying thunder of breakers and roar of escaping steam. When she finally came to rest the paddle-steamer had been driven hard against the pier and those on board were able to scramble ashore without too much difficulty, one of the passengers breaking his leg in the rush to leave the ship. In fact the harbour authorities were completely unaware of what had happened until one of the survivors ran up the pier and alerted some of the pilots. As one of the female passengers was handing her children ashore the

2 Paddle steamer *Brilliant* stranded on the North Pier, Aberdeen, 12 December 1839, an oil painting by J. Faddie (Aberdeen City Arts Department, Art Gallery and Museums).

wreck rolled away from the pier and she was left stranded
aboard along with the second engineer and cook. With
considerable presence of mind the latter quickly made fast a
length of rope around the woman's waist and threw one end to
those on the pier. With the cook and engineer holding the other
end to prevent her from being flung against the pier she was
pulled ashore to be quickly followed by the two remaining
survivors.

As the paddle steamer had been abandoned in such a rush
there had been no time to draw the furnace fires with the result
that the boilers, now empty of water, rapidly over-heated, setting
alight to the wooden hull. The stern was soon burning fiercely
and even though a fire-engine was brought out along the pier it
proved impossible to extinguish the flames. Efforts were then
concentrated on saving the cargo all of which was transferred
ashore before the steamer burned out and broke up. Only two
days after the wreck, several lots of shawls from the cargo, were
advertised for sale by a local firm in the same issue of the
Aberdeen Journal that carried an account of the *Brilliant*'s loss. It
being close to Christmas and the firm run by good Aberdonians
they were presumably anxious to catch the seasonal trade and
turn a little extra profit.

In the first half of the ninteenth century the commonest coastwise cargo was coal, to heat homes, to fuel the ever-increasing
use of steam power and, as a raw material for the embryonic
chemical industry. It has been estimated that as late as the 1820s
the value of this coastwise trade exceeded that of Great Britain's
entire overseas trade. It is therefore not surprising that so many
ships freighted with coal should have been wrecked on the coast
of North East Scotland. The loss of the schooner *Tinker* at
Aberdeen Beach on 22 January 1841 bound for her home port
with a cargo of coal from Newcastle is a typical example. She
had been overtaken by a southerly storm in the bay and had
missed stays while trying to enter the port. With no chance of
wearing back out to sea the schooner was driven ashore opposite
the Bathing Station. The rescue of her crew was notable for the
fact that a majority of the harbour pilots declined, for
unexplained reasons, either to man the lifeboat or assist in her
launch and she had to put to sea with a scratch crew. All of the
schooner's crew were duly rescued with the ship's cat being

brought ashore the following day by a young boy who had gone down to the beach to look at the wreck.

At this time the system of coastal lights which are now taken for granted was very incomplete. For example, although a lighthouse had been established on the Pentland Skerries in 1794 the southern approaches to the Firth remained entirely unlit until the establishment of lighthouses at Noss Head 1849 and Duncansby Head in 1924. In previous years masters of vessels approaching it at night or in poor visibility from the south-east had either to trust to dead-reckoning and attempt a passage or lie off until they could establish their position. Captain Fell, master of the Yarmouth registered schooner *Thomas & Elizabeth* laden with a cargo of gas coal for Dublin, having mistaken Noss Head for Duncansby Head while attempting to pass through the Firth before daybreak on 14 May 1843 ran ashore on Keiss Sands in Sinclair's Bay. As no one on land had seen the schooner go ashore the crew together with the master's wife and child who were also on board had to struggle ashore as best they could in the small-boat. They were unable to save any of their belongings except the clothes they wore and Captain Fell was badly injured on both legs; once on dry land the wretched survivors made their way to a nearby farm for shelter. The schooner soon broke up with the cargo of coal being washed away and buried in the sand.

Fifteen years after the loss of the *Fame*, Mr Craighead of Blackdog farm again played host to the crew of a wrecked ship when the Prussian vessel *Aurora* was driven ashore during a gale on 9 October 1845. She had arrived off the port the previous evening with a cargo of timber from Danzig and after taking a pilot on board had to lie off 'the tide being too far back'. The weather worsened and in a rising south-east gale she was driven to the north and went on the sands about three miles north of Donmouth. A Manby mortar was dispatched from the Bridge of Don Coastguard Station but three attempts to fire a line aboard the stranded vessel failed probably due to the strength of the gale and in the end the crew veered a rope ashore with the aid of cask. A salmon coble manned by some of the local fishermen was hauled out to the ship and those on board brought to safety to be looked after by the hospitable Mr Craighead.

The circumstances of the loss of the wooden paddle-steamer

Velocity at Aberdeen on 25 October 1848 were almost identical to those of the *Brilliant* nine years previously. When she arrived in the bay from Newcastle it was low water and she lay off for about an hour and a half until the leading lights were lit at dusk. It is clear that her master, Captain Stewart, did not appreciate the fact that the lights were lit regardless of the state of the tide and steered for the harbour. The wind, blowing strongly from the south-east combined with a strong fresh in the Dee to produce a heavy sea off the harbour mouth and it was here that the paddle steamer was struck on the starboard quarter by a large wave. Her head was driven to the north and before she could be brought back on course she struck the extreme south-east end of the North Pier. (It should also be noted that it is extremely difficult for a paddle steamer to maintain a steady course in a beam sea with the paddles alternately digging deep in the water or turning uselessly in the air as the vessel rolls. In the confused seas this small ship of only 149 tons gross was probably rolling very heavily with the unfortunate helmsman losing control when just off the harbour mouth).

She struck with such force that her back was broken and she remained lodged fast on the toe of the pier. Although the lifeboat was called out almost as soon as the steamer struck a great deal of time was lost in gathering a volunteer crew. By the time she was launched, the steamer's long boat carrying five of the crew, had managed to get away from the wreck and reach the safety of the harbour. The *Velocity* broke up with the poop deck carrying the master, mate, eight passengers and the remaining five crewmen out into the main channel. They were rescued just in time by the lifeboat which had finally been manned and launched by fishermen who 'conducted the boat nobly, and took the men off the wreck and brought them to land in the most dextrous and seamanlike manner'. It had been impossible to salvage anything from the stranded steamer which broke up and disappeared in less than an hour. Wreckage and cargo were strewn along the Torry side of the river and in spite of guards being set a great deal was stolen under cover of darkness. In a search the following morning the police made several 'painful' discoveries.

It later transpired that no one had full authority to take charge during a rescue operation and the pilots were unwilling to volunteer for the crew claiming they seldom received anything for their efforts. The *Velocity* had been built at Dumbarton in 1821 for the Aberdeen, Leith and Clyde Shipping Company and had run, with the *Brillant*, between Leith, Aberdeen and Inverness before being sold for service with the Aberdeen and Newcastle Steam Navigation Company in 1844.

By the middle of the nineteenth century an increasing number of steamers were coming into service but the bulk of coastwise cargo was still carried by sailing vessels with schooners being far the commonest type. The schooner *Olive* of Goole wrecked at Stonehaven on 4 April 1849 was a typical example. She had been on passage from Hull with a cargo of rails and arrived in Stonehaven Bay at low water. As there was insufficient water on the bar and it was blowing a full easterly gale she was signalled to stand off but tried again to enter when the leading lights were lit at dusk. On this occasion she became embayed and had to drop anchor about a cable's length off the rocks at the north side of the harbour. With the very heavy swell running it was feared that the schooner would either drive under or drag ashore. After some consultation Sheriff Robertson who had taken charge of the rescue operation despatched a messenger to Aberdeen with a letter for the Lord Provost urgently requesting that a tug or lifeboat be sent as neither were stationed at Stonehaven. A lifeboat from a steamer lying in the harbour was loaded aboard a large cart and despatched by road. Unfortunately when it arrived it was found to have been damaged probably by being bumped about in the unsprung cart and there was a considerable delay while repairs were made. The lifeboat finally put off with Captain John Leslie who had accompanied her from Aberdeen acting as coxswain. After being nearly driven back on the shore by the very heavy surf her crew managed to pull alongside the *Olive*.

There was then a long delay while Captain Leslie tried to persuade the schooner's crew to abandon ship. Captain Targoose of the *Olive* refused point blank to leave his ship but finally agreed to send his wife and two young children ashore in the lifeboat. It was then found that she was leaking so badly that it was impossible to keep the water in check and the crew had no choice but to board the schooner for their own safety. As the *Aberdeen Journal* reported they all then went below and 'partook of refreshment'. Those on shore, knowing nothing of these events, were left in great consternation and as dusk fell with still no sign of the lifeboat coming ashore a lookout was posted to warn of any developments. By midnight with the wind having fallen away but the sea continuing to run as high as ever Captain Targoose, on the advice of the lifeboat's crew, decided to run for the harbour and ordered the schooner's top sails to be set. With the master and one of the pilots manning the helm and Captain Leslie conning the ship from the rigging the anchors were weighed. All went well until the *Olive* was close to the harbour entrance when she took the ground in the heavy swell, lost way and broached to before being driven onto rocks at the back of the south pier. Captain Targoose immediately ran below for his wife and two children and sent them ashore one by one securely tied to lines thrown from the rocks. Tragically, two of the men from the lifeboat's crew were swept away and drowned in the surf which was so heavy that the schooner had gone completely to pieces within half an hour of striking. To mark his outstanding courage Captain Leslie was awarded a Silver Medal by the R.N.L.I.

6

The Rise of Steam

North East Scotland was struck by a series of particularly severe northerly gales and blizzards during the second week of January 1852. Roads were blocked by massive drifts up to twenty feet deep with the mail coach between Aberdeen and Elgin being delayed by three days. Considerable damage was done to a new breakwater being constructed at Fraserburgh and as usual coastwise shipping suffered casualties with vessels driven ashore between Findhorn and Cullen but, surprisingly, only one man is known to have been lost. The schooner *Swallow* of Sunderland with a cargo of coal was driven ashore on the sands to the east of the Findhorn estuary during the night of 9 January. As there was no means of bringing the men ashore a cart was despatched to Burghead for a lifeboat and this took five hours to return. In the meantime the unfortunate crew had taken to the rigging and kept shouting for assistance. When the lifeboat was finally launched it capsized no less than three times and it was only due to the extraordinary perseverance of her crew that she reached the schooner and took off the exhausted and frozen men.

On 1 April 1853, forty years to the day on the anniversary of the loss of the *Oscar*, Aberdeen witnessed another disaster at the entrance to the port. The paddle steamer *Duke of Sutherland* belonging to the Aberdeen Steam Navigation Company had sailed two days previously from London with a general cargo and twenty-five passengers. At first the weather remained pleasant but deteriorated steadily and by the time the steamer arrived off Aberdeen it was blowing a full south-easterly gale with heavy rain. As it was low water she had to anchor off during the afternoon until the tide flag was raised shortly after five o'clock. A strong spate coming down the Dee combined with the flood tide to raise a heavy confused sea on the bar, exactly similar conditions to those which had led to the losses of the *Brilliant* and *Velocity*. In a fatal repeat of these tragic events the *Duke of Sutherland* was driven completely off course after being struck on the starboard quarter by a very heavy sea. In spite of five or six men struggling with the helm and the engines being put astern she was completely swept by a second sea which drove her onto the seaward end of the North Pier and extinguished the furnace fires.

She was holed in the vicinity of the boiler room which flooded rapidly with the engineers and stokers having no choice but to abandon their positions. The steamer was then flung broadside-on to the end of the pier before settling on the rocks and starting to break up with the fore-mast soon going over the side. Captain Howling, directing operations with great coolness from the bridge, succeeded in having one of the lifeboats launched just as the bow section broke off and the stern settled further in the water. One of the female passengers was seriously injured when she jumped into the lifeboat while another apparently fainted in the increasing confusion and was swept away with her body being washed up on the beach later. In the very severe swell the lifeboat, in charge of the mate and only containing seven men and a woman, was driven from the side of the stranded steamer before it could be filled and drifted safely through the surf to the beach. The harbour lifeboat had been launched within twenty minutes of the steamer going aground but having been driven against the wreck and damaged, she had to make for the safety of the beach carrying only fifteen survivors.

This still left some thirty people on the rapidly disintegrating wreck sheltering around the starboard paddle-box. In an attempt to fire a line aboard a number of Dennett's rockets and lifelines were obtained from the Round House but because of the inexperience of those using them it took well over twenty attempts before one actually fell across the wreck. After that a pier hawser was drawn aboard but with no proper cradle available one had to be improvised from a box that had floated free from the wreck. It became obvious however after the first person (one of the female passengers) had been brought ashore that this was unsatisfactory and large rope slings were

3 The rescue of the passengers and crew of the paddle steamer *Duke of Sutherland* ashore on the North Pier, Aberdeen, 1 April 1853, from a lithograph by 'W.E.' (Aberdeen City Arts Department, Art Gallery and Museums).

substituted instead. At this point the whip became entangled and
Captain Howling, having just been knocked down by a wildly
swinging quarter boat while saving one of the female passengers
entangled in the stern netting, tried to free it but fell off the warp
into the sea and drowned in full view of his brother who was on
the pier.

Simultaneously a salmon coble manned by some seamen and
the steamer's second mate, Peter Ligertwood, who had been
brought ashore in the harbour lifeboat managed to put off from
the beach and pick up several people who had been washed off
the poop of the wrecked steamer. On the way back to the beach
the coble fouled some nearby salmon nets and capsized, only one
of the crew of six men reaching the shore alive. It was then that
the hero of the disaster emerged. The Chief Steward, Duncan
Christie, took charge of directing rescue operations on the
stranded paddle-steamer and with a mixture of extraordinary
effort, encouragement and the occasional threat succeeded in
safely sending ashore the twenty or so people who were still
aboard the midships section. Finally, having ensured that all of
the survivors had reached the pier safely Christie left the wreck
with a knife clenched between his teeth in case the rope pulling
him ashore became entangled. In fact this was exactly what did
happen and he had to cut himself free just as he reached the pier.

Because of the heavy loss of life Aberdeen Harbour
Commissioners immediately appointed a full-time paid crew
for the lifeboat and ordered an inquiry into the state and
availability of the rescue equipment held at the harbour. It
emerged that the lifeboat had arrived alongside the casualty only
half an hour after she struck but had been so badly damaged by
floating debris during the rescue that she was unable to return to
the stranded steamer. Severe problems were caused by nearby
salmon stake-nets which entangled some of those swept off the
steamer and fouled the coble while it was alongside the steamer.
The delay in the use of the Dennett rockets was found to be due
to a combination of inexperience, heavy spray soaking the rocket
fuses and misguided interference from the huge crowd of
onlookers. On a happier note the Chief Steward's bravery was
awarded with £5 and a gold medal by the Shipwrecked
Fishermen and Mariners' Royal Benevolent Fund.

Even though steam was rapidly superseding sail by the middle of the ninteenth century sailing vessels were still extensively used in the transportation of bulk cargoes such as coal, grain and timber. The last named in particular was imported in huge quantities from abroad, domestic supplies being quite inadequate to satisfy the demands of the Industrial Revolution which by now was in full swing. The Dutch galliot *De Leeuw* of Schiedam bound for Liverpool with a cargo of Memel timber in late November 1856 was a typical example. In order to avoid the Pentland Firth, Captain Ridder, her master, decided to sail via the Caledonian Canal as his ship was of only 200 tons burden. Being unfamiliar with the Moray Firth he dropped anchor off Nairn on the evening of 28 November in a north-north-westerly gale and picked up a pilot the following day. After a further night off Nairn the anchor was weighed the following morning but it was found that insufficent sail could be set to clear the western point of the 'Old Bar' off the Culbin shore. The anchor was dropped a second time but by this time the galliot was close inshore on poor holding ground and she finally dragged ashore on the Bar during the evening. By the time the *De Leeuw* was inspected by a Lloyds agent at the beginning of the following week she was completely water-logged and it was feared that she would become a total wreck. In the event and with the assistance of some local fishermen Captain Ridder successfully refloated his ship a few days later.

In spite of the rapid strides made in the introduction of steampower at sea there was no equivalent advance made in the improvement of navigational aids available to mariners. Thus, in poor visibility watch-keeping officers had only a compass, leadline and some form of patent log to rely on when shaping a course. The thick fogs which could form off the north-east coast were a particular hazard at all seasons of the year. By 1859 a scheduled steamer service between Aberdeen, Wick and the Northern Isles was well established. The wooden paddler *Duke of Richmond* owned by the Aberdeen, Leith and Clyde Shipping Company ran between Leith and Wick via Aberdeen. Having embarked 114 passengers and laden with a cargo of fish and livestock she left Wick on the forenoon of 7 October 1859 bound for Aberdeen. By the time she arrived off the port early the following morning thick fog had reduced visibility to virtually nil. Although the pier lights were just visible Captain Geddes decided to lie off till daylight. As he had been on the bridge all night he turned in having first given strict instructions to the mate to keep the ship well off the land. About two hours later with the fog still as thick as ever breakers were sighted dead ahead and in spite of the engines being put full astern the steamer ran hard aground on the beach at Blackdog north of Aberdeen.

There was something of a panic amongst the passengers who crowded into the ship's boats and demanded that they be sent ashore at once. Order was restored with difficulty before one of the ship's boats could be launched and initially pulled away from the shore in the pitch darkness before reaching the beach safely. It was then discovered that it was possible to wade ashore and the children aboard were carried to dry land on men's backs. Fortunately the weather remained moderate and there were no casualties amongst the passengers and crew. However this did not prevent the *Orcadian* which obviously had its own set of priorities from reporting the loss of the *Duke of Richmond* under banner headlines which included 'Thirty Cattle Lost'. These unfortunate animals were part of a consignment of livestock stowed between decks which were trapped and drowned. As soon as news of the stranding reached Aberdeen tugs and lifeboats were dispatched to the scene together with one hundred carpenters from Hall's shipyard. In spite of most of the cargo being removed and the arrival of an additional party of carpenters the steamer remained stuck fast even at high water and efforts were concentrated on salvaging the cargo. Although built on the Clyde in 1838 the steamer had received a total overhaul just a year before she stranded and her loss was a severe financial blow to her owners.

The Aberdeen, Leith and Clyde Shipping Company continued to suffer disastrous losses when their iron screw steamer *Hamburg* struck Scotstown Head in poor visibility and a heavy gale early on the morning of 12 October 1862. She had sailed from Kirkwall bound for Aberdeen with a consignment of livestock and two passengers again under the command of Captain Geddes. As she had gone ashore at high water it was possible for the livestock and passengers to be landed at low water without loss. Three tugs dispatched from Aberdeen attempted to tow the steamer off but she was firmly embedded on a rock which had penetrated her hull by about six feet. The ship was completely tidal with the pumps unable to cope and she finally had to be abandoned as a total loss.

Astonishingly the company lost another vessel the following year when their iron paddle steamer *Prince Consort* struck the North Pier at Aberdeen in March of the following year. By any standards this ship had an extremely chequered career. She had been built at Port Glasgow and entered service with the company in 1858. For her size of 623 tons gross she was, unlike most of her contemporaries, extremely powerful with her engines developing some 300 HP. The ship was also rigged for sail, a necessary precaution, as early marine engines were somewhat temperamental. Her first accident occurred in September 1860 when she struck Noss Head in thick fog while trying to make a landfall at Wick, losing her bow sprit and figure-head besides 'being much cut and shattered about the bow'. The passengers who were below at the time rushed on deck in a panic and a boat was lowered before it was realised that the *Prince Consort* was not holed below the waterline and in no danger of sinking. At the request of one of the passengers a clergyman offered up what was described as an impressive prayer for their deliverance. Although seriously damaged the steamer was able to continue her voyage to Lerwick after calling at Wick.

Her stranding at Aberdeen on 11 March 1863 was a great deal more serious. The paddle steamer had sailed early that morning from Leith on her scheduled run to Aberdeen. While trying to enter the port later the same day in a south-east wind and ebb tide the steamer yawed violently after being struck on the quarter by a large wave and grounded on the North Pier. Fortunately assistance was soon at hand and all of the passengers and crew were taken off by Manby lifesaving apparatus without suffering major injuries. However the master of the tug *Hawk* had his leg broken while trying to pass a line to the stranded steamer. According to the *Orkney Herald* one of those saved had been a steward on three previous ships lost by the Aberdeen,Leith and Clyde. Although it was possible to salvage a considerable quantity of cargo from the forward section she broke in two and the stern sank in deep water. In spite of this she was purchased by Messrs Catto, Thomson and Company, refloated, and completely reconstructed 'on the most approved principles' before being sold back to her original owners.

Some idea of the problems that sailing vessels could encounter during a voyage are vividly illustrated by the fate of the Shields registered barque *Pasha*. She sailed from Quebec at the end of August 1864 with a cargo of timber for Seaham on what the *Peterhead Sentinel* described with major understatement as a 'rather unfortunate passage'. After two months at sea she had had to put into Stornoway on 26 October and lie there wind-bound till 3 November. Because of adverse winds she then had to shelter successively at Scrabster, Cromarty and Fraserburgh. By now the barque was leaking badly and she had to put back to Cromarty several times before leaving there at the end of December. With the crew by now completely exhausted from continually manning the pumps the captain was forced to put into Peterhead and telegraphed the owners for a tug. On instructions the master shipped more hands to help with the pumps and sailed on New Year's Day but put back again when a gale blew up. Finally on the evening of 3 January while lying in the South Bay waiting for a tug one of the anchor cables parted in a south-south-west gale and the barque started to drift down on the rocks of South Head. As it proved impossible to set enough canvas to clear the land the crew abandoned ship in the boats leaving the *Pasha* to drive ashore. By the next morning she had broken in two and become a total wreck with the crew having lost all their belongings.

Although steam power continued its inexorable rise sailing vessels continued to be built in large numbers, some being of substantial size like the 1,381 register ton iron full-rigged ship *Leila* of Liverpool. She had been launched as the *Dr Gall* from the yards of Richardson, Duck and Company, Stockton, in June 1864 for James Baines and Company of Liverpool. In November shortly before completion she was sold to Stuart and Douglas of Liverpool and renamed the *Leila*. Under the command of Captain C. Fairbairn she sailed from Shields on 2 January bound for Calcutta on 2 January with a cargo of coal. Apart from the crew of twenty seven men she also carried a North Sea pilot. Nothing more was heard from her until large amounts of wreckage were washed ashore on the Caithness coast in the vicinity of Wick. There was some confusion as to the identity of the wreck, as apart from a name board with *Leila* in gilt letters coming ashore a parcel of lifebuoys addressed to – *Gall*, North Shields, was also recovered. There was no sign of any survivors and it was presumed that she had gone ashore under the cliffs south of Noss Head. The season had been a particularly stormy one with the coast being swept by a series of severe easterly gales.

On her last voyage the *Prince Consort* sailed from Granton in dense fog on the evening of 10 May 1867. She carried seventy-three passengers and a large cargo of merchant goods in addition to mails for Orkney and Shetland. The fact that she was carrying mails was given as the principal reason for her sailing in such poor visibility. All went well until about a quarter to five the following morning when the master, Captain Robert Parrot, still unable to see the shore ordered the mate to take a sounding. This was incorrectly reported as thirty-six fathoms and would have put the steamer at least four miles off shore. In fact the mate had used a old lead line that had broken at the twenty fathom mark, a new lead having been bent on there, and he had made a simple error in calculating the depth. The true sounding of sixteen fathoms put the steamer less than a mile offshore. Believing that he had plenty of sea room Captain Parrot changed his course to the north and ordered the lead to be cast again. Just as this was being done breakers were sighted on the port bow and in spite of the helm being ordered hard a-port the *Prince Consort* struck the Hasman Rock about two miles south of Girdle Ness.

There was little wind but the steamer bumped badly in the heavy ground swell before settling on a rock off Burnbanks, Cove. The passengers below, awakened by the impact, rushed on deck half dressed or in their night-attire. A lifeboat, launched with the aid of some of the deck passengers, filled when it was dropped bow first into the water. Fortunately, a second one was successfully launched and made for the shore at Burnbanks with a dozen survivors aboard. The noise of escaping steam and shouts of the passengers alerted the salmon fishers at Altens and several cobles put off to investigate. In the heavy ground swell the survivors were taken off with considerable difficulty one of the passengers having his leg crushed between a coble's gunwhale and the side of the steamer. One coble had her bows stove in but managed to reach the shore safely with her load of survivors. By this time the *Prince Consort* had started to break up and Captain Parrot who had directed rescue operations with great coolness had to be forcibly removed from the poop which almost immediately broke off and sank.

Most of the passengers and crew escaped with only the clothes they wore and lost all their possessions. One, a Major Yates, bound for Kirkwall to take over as adjutant of the Orkney Volunteers, lost all his household furniture while another, returning from New Zealand, lost an estimated £300 in gold coin. The wreck broke up and huge amounts of wreckage and cargo came ashore with a considerable amount of passengers' baggage being recovered. Some of the survivors were looked after at the Altens fishing station while others either caught a train at the nearby Cove railway station or found their own way into Aberdeen.

At the subsequent Board of Trade Inquiry it was established that the principal cause for the stranding of the *Prince Consort* was due to the incorrect sounding reported by the mate. Captain Parrot who had commanded the *Prince Consort* throughout her adventurous career was cleared of recklessly hazarding his ship and handed back his masters' certificate. The *Orkney Herald* reported that 'the decision of the court was received with loud applause by the audience'.

Previous shipwrecks paled into insignificance with the stranding of the Bremen registered steamer *Union* off Rattray Head early on the morning of 29 November 1870. She was carrying 310 passengers, mostly emigrants, plus a crew of 112 and was bound for New York with mail and general cargo which included 1,200 canaries. At that time France and Prussia were at war and Captain Dreyer, fearing that his ship might be seized by French warships altered course to keep close the British coast. At about ten o'clock at night when off Buchan Ness one of the bearings started to overheat and the engines had to stopped. Repairs took about two and a half hours but during this time and unknown to the captain the steamer was being carried steadily north by the tide. By the time the engines were restarted, at about one o'clock in the morning, the steamer was close inshore and she grounded shortly afterwards on Rattray Briggs (which at that time were unlit). After bumping several times the *Union* stuck fast.

In spite of the crew firing distress rockets and lighting flares no one ashore realised that anything was amiss until the stranded steamer was spotted at daylight by coastguards. On board the passengers and crew were busily baling and pumping the ship in a futile attempt to keep the water down. Fortunately the weather remained calm and when it became obvious that there was no chance of the steamer being refloated the ship's lifeboats were launched. Under the direction of the coastguard the crew landed the passengers at the small fishing settlement of Botany (also known as Rattray Fish-town). Once ashore the unfortunate passengers huddled on the beach with whatever possessions that they had been able to save and waited for assistance. The task of providing shelter for the four hundred or so survivors fell on the shoulders of the Consul for the North German Federation. Some were given shelter at Middleton of Rattray and the farm also provided tea for the people on the beach. Others were taken in gigs and carts provided by James Reid's Royal Horse Bazaar to Peterhead where large crowds gathered to watch their arrival.

The weather continued fine for the next few days which allowed a considerable quantity of baggage and freight, including the 1,200 canaries to be brought ashore. Although two tugs were sent from Aberdeen it proved impossible for them to get near the steamer and she broke up in a northerly gale. With huge amounts of wreck coming ashore a guard of twelve constables under the command of Major Ross, Chief Constable of Aberdeenshire, was posted along the beach. In spite of this a considerable amount of pilfering took place and a further ten constables were sent from Aberdeen. 'Certain parties,' reported the *Buchan Observer*, 'found making free with articles from the wreck' appeared in Aberdeen Sheriff Court and were 'punished rather smartly'. A fortnight after the stranding the shipwrecked passengers were taken aboard a specially chartered steamer to continue their voyage to America.

In spite of the increasing number of steamships lost on the north-east coast it was still sailing vessels that continued to suffer severely in any prolonged southerly gales. At the end of February 1874 the coasts around Scotland experienced a particulerly severe storm which caused widespread damage inland and numerous casualties at sea. At Aberdeen the Stonehaven lifeboat which had been trying to assist a vessel in distress capsized off the North Pier with four of her crew drowned. The tragedy had begun on the afternoon of 28

February when the Blyth registered barque *Grace Darling* was sighted off Stonehaven labouring heavily and displaying distress signals. The lifeboat *St George* was launched and followed the barque which bore away to the north before the storm. The harbour authorities at Aberdeen had been alerted by a telegram from Stonehaven but for unexplained reasons the lifeboat was not launched until the barque had passed the port. Once off Aberdeen the barque made no attempt to enter but the distress signal was hauled down and she sailed on northwards.

In the meantime the Stonehaven lifeboat had arrived off the harbour, the sail was lowered and her crew took to the oars. All went well until she was between the North Pier and South Breakwater when she broached to and capsized in the huge swell. By the time she had righted six of the crew were in the water with the coxswain clinging to the bow. One man floated towards the Breakwater apparently stunned while the four others were carried away to the north. In spite of strenuous efforts by the six men in the lifeboat she was driven by the huge swell round the back of the North Pier where they managed to scramble ashore along with the coxswain who was still in the water clinging to the bows. By this time the harbour lifeboat had been launched and set off northwards to try to pick up the four men who had been last seen floating towards the mouth of the River Don. In the event they succeeded in picking up only one man while another was rescued from the surf by the crowd who linked hands to form a human chain but was found to be dead by the time medical assistance arrived. One body came ashore that night but two lifeboatmen remained unaccounted for.

Meanwhile the *Grace Darling* continued to drive before the storm passing Peterhead about ten o'clock that night. The authorities there had also been warned by a telegram from Stonehaven but there was considerable delay before the lifeboat could be launched as both first and second coxswains were absent. Apart from that, in a misguided attempt to help, a mob many of whom were drunk, dropped the front wheels of the lifeboat carriage onto the deck of a vessel lying in the harbour wasting even more time. By the time the lifeboat finally put off the barque had passed the harbour and in spite of searching for three hours in a pitch black stormy night no trace could be found and she had to return to Peterhead. It was only the following day when the sole survivor was discovered on the sands just south of St Combs that her fate became known. From him it was gathered that the master of the barque despairing of being rescued decided to run his ship ashore and hope that the crew would be rescued at daylight. In the event this ended in disaster with the *Grace Darling* breaking up almost immediately. All of her crew of eleven men were lost apart from the sole survivor who reached the beach clinging to a piece of wreckage.

7

The Great Storms of 1875 and 1876

The terrible losses suffered at sea in the great storm of January 1800 were completely dwarfed by those which occurred during the appalling gales which struck the east coast of Great Britain in October 1875 and December 1876. On the north-east coast of Scotland losses were particularly severe. In terms of ships wrecked and lives lost in December 1876 precise totals will never be known as several of the casualties remain unidentified and even such an authoritative source as *Lloyds List* was unable to give a complete record of events, so overwhelming was the magnitude of the disaster. Although local newspapers provided a wealth of information it has proved exceptionally difficult to discover the precise order in which the casualties occurred. The *Aberdeen Weekly Journal*, an otherwise excellent source, gives differing days and times for some wrecks in the same issue! Bearing these qualifications in mind it would appear that at least fifteen vessels and fifty-six lives were lost in October 1875 while the totals for December 1876 are thirty-one vessels wrecked or sunk with at least one hundred and fifty lives lost. So far as can be established all of the vessels lost were sailing ships with the majority belonging to Scandinavian owners. The losses for October 1875 and December 1876 are summarised in Appendices 1 and 2.

In the storm of 1875 a south-easterly sprang up on the morning of 14 October and continued with increasing violence till the end of the following week when it finally moderated. The huge seas which hammered on the coast caused considerable damage to the harbours at Stonehaven and Aberdeen. In the case of the latter a sixty ton block of masonry was torn from the

North Pier and later discovered one hundred yards away in the bed of the navigation channel. The full sequence of losses has been related in detail as it vividly illustrates how completely sailing vessels were at the mercy of wind and weather.

The first lives to be lost were those of seven men from the brig *Johann Cornelius* of Rostock which had been abandoned about twenty four miles off Buchan Ness early on the morning of 15 October. She had sailed in ballast from King's Lynn on 8 October and was picked up by a tug off Hartlepool for towing to Shields. Before reaching her destination the tow rope parted when the weather rapidly deteriorated and Captain Fraedtlandt decided to run for the Baltic. When the brig was about eighty miles off the Norwegian coast the wind backed and strengthened and she was forced to run before the weather labouring heavily and taking in water. She was finally thrown on her beam-ends by a heavy sea early on the morning of 15 October and the crew abandoned ship in the longboat. Having made a landfall at the Ward of Cruden the boat broached to and capsized in the massive surf about one hundred yards from the beach throwing the crew into the water. Captain Fraedtlandt, the only man wearing a lifejacket, was the sole survivor with everyone else being drowned. No trace was found of the brig which is presumed to have sunk shortly after being abandoned.

Four days later with the storm continuing unabated from the south-south-east the Prussian schooner *Auguste* of Stettin was driven on the rocks at Longhaven south of Buchan Ness. She had sailed the previous week from Christiana (Oslo) with a cargo of battens for Thurso and after experiencing severe weather in the North Sea her master had tried to shelter at Peterhead. Having been unable to enter the port she tacked about the coast but the captain misjudged the strength of the flood tide and she struck the rocks at Longhaven during the night. Her crew of three were flung into the water and the eighteen year old cook drowned in the surf. The master and mate managed to scramble ashore and took refuge on a ledge in the cliffs where they remained all night soaked by spray and completely unprotected from the storm. They were discovered the next day and rescued by some local men with the aid of ropes. By this time the schooner had broken up completely with little worth saving from the wreckage.

On the following evening (20 October) another schooner was sighted in distress off Salthouse Head just south of Peterhead, before she disappeared in a squall. A few days later a name board painted with the words *Julie Gaso* was picked up on the shore close to where the schooner had been last sighted but there was no sign of any of her crew. Next morning with the storm still continuing to blow unabated, coastguards at Muchalls sighted another schooner close inshore driving north with no hope of weathering the coast. The rocket apparatus was immediately brought out and rushed north to where it was thought she would strike. Some of her sails then blew out and she drove onto an offshore rock. With the rocket brigade helpless spectators the schooner almost immediately went to pieces with no chance of any one surviving in the terrible surf. Later that day the ship's papers and clock together with a quantity of apples were found on the shore and identified her as the *John Murray* of Exeter which had sailed with a crew of four.

Unknown to those ashore the Shields brig *Dorothy Jobson* foundered off Stonehaven the same afternoon (21 October) with the loss of all hands. The disaster only came to light the following weekend when a bottle containing papers together with a name board and part of a ship's boat were found on the beach at Cowie. The papers consisted of brief notes from two of the crew who, realising that they would shortly perish, were bidding farewell to family and friends. They also revealed that early on the day she sank the brig had been struck by a huge sea off Arbroath which brought down the foretop mast, carried away the wheel and washed the master and mate overboard. Attempts to launch the ship's boat failed when it was swamped and a makeshift raft was swept away before anyone could get onto it. Later the same day a schooner hove in sight but was unable to render any assistance because of the terrible conditions leaving the survivors to their fate.

During that night another Shields brig was lost with all hands on rocks south of Stonehaven in the vicinity of Dunnottar Castle. Her clock, which had stopped at ten o'clock and some of the ship's papers came ashore and identified her as the *John and Isabella Smith* bound from Gelle (?Gevle) to Sunderland with a cargo of battens and a crew of seven. Early the next morning (22 October) the Swedish brig *Superior* of Kalmar went to pieces on the cliffs south of Muchalls with the loss of her crew believed to number about eight men. No one on land saw the tragedy which was only discovered when a log book and clock were recovered from wreckage cast ashore. A little later that same morning with the wind blowing storm force south-east the Norwegian barque *Hjack*, fourteen days out from Sunderland with a cargo of coal for Christiania drove ashore on the beach two miles north of Scotstown Head. She was spotted at first light by coastguards on watch at Rattray Head and the rocket brigade immediately called out. Because the barque lay so far offshore and on account of the storm force winds it proved impossible in spite of repeated attempts, to get a line aboard. With all available rocket lines soaked and unserviceable the Peterhead rocket apparatus was brought up and a line finally thrown over the rigging. The Peterhead lifeboat was also called out but, because of the huge seas running off the port, could not be launched. It was therefore brought overland along the main turnpike to the scene of the wreck. Fortunately by the time she arrived her services were not required as all of the barque's crew had been safely brought ashore.

A few hours later, in the late forenoon, a schooner was spotted off Girdle Ness running north before the wind and labouring heavily. She made no attempt to enter the harbour and with the Aberdeen lifeboat (which had been manned and kept in readiness) following, grounded on the beach just north of the Bathing Station. To the loud cheers of the crowd which had assembled, the lifeboat quickly took off the crew of five. The schooner, which proved to be the *Isabella Miller* of Colchester, described 'as a staunch Scottish built vessel', in ballast from London for Hartlepool, received little damage and it was expected that she would be refloated when the weather moderated.

Early that afternoon the Prussian schooner *Baumeister Kraeft* lost way while trying to enter Peterhead harbour and stranded on rocks close to the harbour entrance. As she was rolling violently and likely to break up at any moment a pilot boat was quickly manned and put off to save the schooner's crew. At the first attempt three men were taken off with great difficulty and landed. It was while trying to bring off the remaining three men that the pilot boat was struck by the schooner which was still rolling violently, and capsized throwing the crew into the water. By great good fortune they all managed to scramble on board the stranded schooner to await their rescue. In desperation three men on shore put off in a rowing boat and succeeded in taking aboard three of the stranded rescuers but disaster struck and it was swamped just off the rocks. The six men struggled in the heavy surf with huge waves breaking over them. It was only through the gallant efforts of some spectators on the rocks that four of those in the water were dragged ashore alive with one of them dying almost immediately. The two others, having been completely exhausted by their struggle to stay afloat in the heavy seas, drowned before assistance could reach them. In spite of this disaster another pilot boat was manned and successfully landed all of the men still stranded on the schooner. It transpired that the *Baumeister Kraeft* had sailed a month previously from Memel with a cargo of wood for Shields and during that time had been driven about the Baltic and North Sea by storms.

Later in the afternoon with the storm continuing to blow unabated the Danish sloop *Nathalia Jacobsina* with a cargo of pit props for Bo'ness tried to run for the shelter of Peterhead harbour. Just off the entrance she was caught by a huge wave and flung on the rocks close to the wreck of *Baumeister Kraeft*. The lifeboat, by now manned and ready because of the loss of life earlier that afternoon had the sloop's crew safely ashore only ten minutes after she struck. Her captain, Mogens Andersen, reported that on the previous day he had fallen in with a dismasted barque whose crew had taken to their boat. In spite of repeated attempts to get a line to the survivors, about a dozen men in all, they were unable to make it fast being either in the last stages of exhaustion or dead in the bottom of the boat. Captain Andersen, finally and with great reluctance, had to give up the rescue attempt and run for Peterhead in the gathering darkness. The barque was almost certainly the *Behrend* of Memel which drove ashore derelict about two hours after the sloop had struck, at Waterhaven, a mile and a half south of Buchan Ness. She was identified from part of a ship's boat (possibly the one which contained the doomed survivors) washed ashore further south. Although huge numbers of logs from her cargo came ashore there were no signs of any survivors and no bodies were ever recovered. The *Nathalia Jacobsina* did not break up and was refloated once the storm had subsided and towed into Peterhead for repairs.

Early on the morning of Saturday 23 October coastguards at Collieston discovered a brigantine ashore on the Sands of Forvie about a mile north of the Ythan mouth. Although the wind had moderated considerably there was still a very heavy sea running with no chance of any lifeboat being able to rescue the survivors who had gathered on the bow section. The discovery caused considerable consternation as the Board of Trade had, for reasons best known to itself, removed the rocket apparatus from the Collieston Coastguard Station the previous year. Fortunately an old set still remained and this was pressed into service while an urgent telegram was sent to the coastguard station at Donmouth asking for their set to be sent north immediately. The brigantine which proved to be the *Olga* of Nyborg, in the then Russian province of Finland, had broken in two with both masts going over the side. Using the old apparatus a line was fired to the men on the bow section and four survivors were brought ashore before the equipment gave way and rescue operations had to be suspended. The Donmouth rocket apparatus arrived soon afterwards having covered the thirteen and a half miles by road in an hour. Their first rocket landed a line on the bow section but it fouled on floating wreckage after four of the crew had been brought off. When on the point of firing another rocket the officer in charge saw that the men on the wreck had managed to reach the stern section which was lying a great deal further out of the water than the bow. With the hawser tied to the highest point of the wreck's bulwarks and thus keeping it free of floating wreckage, the five remaining men were taken ashore. The captain reported that the brigantine had gone ashore the previous night with the wretched crew having to spend the hours of darkness clinging to the wreck without shelter and being constantly soaked by succeeding waves.

The fourteenth casualty of the storm was the French schooner *Mediateur* which went on the beach at Spey Bay close to the Boar's Head early on the morning of 23 October. Having sailed from Antwerp on 15 October in ballast for Sunderland she was blown completely off course by the storm. Her crew was saved by the local rocket brigade with the assistance of some men from Branderburgh and cared for by the Shipwrecked Mariners

Society in Lossiemouth. Towards the end of the month the Norwegian brig *Minnie* drifted ashore derelict at Whinnyfold, Cruden Bay, with no sign of her crew.

Without doubt the storm of 22-23 December 1876 was the most terrible in terms of losses at sea that the North East of Scotland ever experienced. Apart from the known casualties huge quantities of unidentified wreckage were also cast ashore along the entire coastline so the totals for losses must be regarded as a minimum figure. At its height it blew Force 12 from the east and was accompanied by snow and latterly thunder and lightning. The surge in Aberdeen harbour was so severe that at one point one of the retaining chains on the lockgates parted and they had to be opened to prevent further damage. At low water most of the shipping lying in the dock settled on the bottom fortunately without sustaining any damage. Incredibly, and probably in desperation, some vessels managed to enter the port on 23 December even though huge seas were running in the navigation channel.

From the wreckage of one vessel cast ashore at Stonehaven shortly after daybreak on 22 December it was obvious that she was in a deplorable condition and should never have been at sea. She had broken up at once with the loss of all on board and only identified as the barque *Johanna* of Danzig when her log was recovered from the beach at Cowie. She apparently carried a woman passenger as some items of female clothing were also found. Parts of her timbers were so rotten that it was possible to pick them to pieces by hand. The papers recovered included a deposition made eight years previously by the captain when he had to put into Stornoway for repairs as the *Johanna* was in an unseaworthy state and making water.

Later that morning a brig, labouring heavily and obviously in distress, was sighted off Belhelvie. As it was clear that she would shortly be driven ashore by the storm which was still blowing furiously, a Mr Leith who farmed locally, sent one of his farmhands to warn the coastguards at Belhelvie and set off himself on horseback for the Donmouth station to summon the rocket apparatus. By the time the apparatus had arrived the brig had grounded well offshore at Eigie and a boat containing four survivors had been swamped in the surf. In spite of heroic efforts by two of the Belhelvie coastguards and some salmon fishers who waded out to try to save one of the survivors who had managed to stay afloat he was swept away and disappeared. The brig, which proved to be the *William* of Mandal, did not break up and a rocket line was fired over her in case any survivors still remained aboard. In fact the only survivor was the ship's dog which swam ashore unseen and turned up at a nearby salmon fishers' bothy.

Later that day just as darkness was falling a vessel was seen in distress off Newtonhill and the coastguards turned to with the rocket apparatus. Most of the inhabitants from Muchalls and Skateraw turned out as well and as no horses were available helped drag the rocket carriage along the cliffs. It was to no avail as by the time they arrived the vessel had broken up with only a few spars showing. Her nameboard was cast ashore the following morning which identified her as the Prussian galliot *Christian Marie*. In the forenoon the body of the master lashed to the mizzen rigging was recovered. He was dressed in his best uniform and had a gold watch and a letter addressed to Captain B. Hadum in his pockets. It is clear that he had realised that there was no chance of survival and had resolved to meet his end bravely.

Away to the north as night fell the crew of the Russian barque *Au Revoir* were losing a battle to weather the Caithness coast. She was sighted close inshore off Wick at about four o'clock when the rocket brigade were summoned. Although she managed to clear Noss Head the barque was finally driven ashore on the north side of Sinclair's Bay close to Keiss Castle. In spite of a line being successfully fired aboard her crew seemed quite unable to work the gear and three of them jumped overboard to be pulled from the surf more dead than alive. The eight remaining men clung throughout the night to the rigging of the wrecked ship which by some miracle did not break up. By dawn the *Au Revoir* had been driven further inshore and they jumped overboard one by one to be rescued by a crowd of onlookers.

By the time all of the crew of the *Au Revoir* had reached safety the Prussian schooner *Emelie* of Wolgast which had anchored in Sinclair's Bay overnight dragged ashore at Ackergill. There was a considerable delay while rockets were brought from Wick but as it was low water and the schooner was close inshore the crew did not appear to be in any immediate danger. It was only with the sixth and last rocket that a line finally landed on the schooner. Even then her crew appeared more interested in roping up their sea-chests and could only be persuaded with difficulty to haul the hawser and whips aboard. When, through some misunderstanding it was slackened off, the whips parted in the surf and only the hawser remained. Impatient of further delays some of the crowd of spectators launched a coble and hauled themselves out along the hawser to the stranded schooner. On the return trip with three of the crew aboard the coble broached to in the huge surf and capsized throwing everyone into the sea. Of the twelve men in the boat only six reached the shore alive with three of the rescuers and the three men from the schooner drowning. One of the survivors still aboard the *Emelie* tried to drag himself along the hawser and in spite of being washed off was rescued alive from the breakers. With all rockets fired the Scarfskerry Life Saving Apparatus was summoned but by the time it arrived the schooner had broken up and the three men still aboard drowned.

During that morning three ships had been driven ashore in the vicinity of Rattray Head but by some miracle all of the crews reached shore safely. One of these, the Dutch galliot *Tijsiena* having been disabled by the loss of her bowsprit at sea, drove ashore at Charleston, St Combs. After four rockets failed to put a line aboard, a yawl was manned by local fishermen and they managed to take off the crew of three men and a boy. The yawl filled as it was returning to the shore but the crowd ashore joined hands to form a human chain and pulled everyone to safety. The boy had had a particularly lucky escape, having been washed from the galliot's rigging by a wave; he was bundled into the galley for safety by the captain who then had to run aloft again before the next wave washed him away.

By the afternoon the wind had moderated considerably but huge seas were still running on the coast. In Spey Bay a barque labouring heavily was spotted close inshore and steering westwards. By the time she passed Lossiemouth at three o'clock she was seen to be flying a distress flag which was lowered after Stotfield Head was cleared. For totally unexplained reasons the barque then altered course towards the land, the captain presumably having the intention of running the ship ashore but apparently unaware that he was heading straight for the Halliman Skerries. The lifeboat was immediately taken out of the shed on her carriage by some of the crowd who had gathered and dragged to Stotfield Bay. By this time the barque had struck the eastern end of the Skerries and was being swept by huge waves which were breaking as high as the mastheads. Showing great moral courage the coxswain decided, on the advice of the Committee members present, not to launch the lifeboat as night was falling and there was not the slightest chance of her surviving the terrible conditions. In fact it seems unlikely that the lifeboat would have been reached the stranded barque in time as the masts where the crew had taken refuge went over the side within half an hour of her striking. The decision caused bitter controversy in the town but the coxswain showed sound judgement in not sacrificing his crew in some futile rescue attempt. By the following day conditions had improved sufficently for the lifeboat to be launched but the barque had broken up completely and there was no sign of any survivors. It was not until several days later that she was identified as the *Alexander* of Danzig.

By the end of the storm it must have been painfully obvious to the most prejudiced ship-owner that the days of sailing vessels were numbered. The volumes of freight which had to be carried to support the massive industrial expansion of the latter half of the nineteenth century required a far more dependable type of transportation and the rise of steam power was therefore assured. The storm also demonstrated the wisdom of the recently introduced 'Plimsoll Act' which required, amongst other things, that British registered ships pass a rigorous annual survey. Many of the vessels which failed to pass this survey were sold to Continental owners and it is interesing to note that none of the positively identified wrecks which occurred during the storm on the north-east coast of Scotland were British.

8

'An Accident of a Serious Nature'

Although there were disasters in the last quarter of the nineteenth century they were never on the same scale as the terrible losses of 1875 and 1876. There was a huge increase in the number of steam powered vessels which could cope far more readily with severe weather conditions. For all that, sail was a long time a-dying, with coasting vessels such as ketches and schooners continuing to carry low value bulk cargoes around the British Isles until well into the twentieth century. Some, like the schooner *Lowestoft Merchant* of Lyme Regis, were owned by their masters. This little ship (she was only some 61 tons register) had sailed with a crew of three from Sunderland in the middle of June 1877 bound for northern Scotland with a cargo of coal. Off the south coast of the Moray Firth the weather worsened unexpectedly and by the afternoon of 22 June it was blowing a full gale from the north-east. With heavy seas running and an onshore wind all sails were set on the schooner in an effort to weather the coast off Speymouth. The consequences were disastrous. The press of canvas was so great that the masts broke and went over the side and the schooner was driven before the gale onto the sand bank known as the Boar's Head about two miles east of Lossiemouth. In spite of being launched almost immediately the lifeboat's crew had great difficulty in making any headway against the very heavy swell and only reached the casualty after rowing for an hour and a half. They found the schooner which was being swept clean by heavy seas deserted with no sign of the crew who had either been washed overboard or had taken to the long boat and drowned when it swamped. When some woman's clothing was picked up from the wreck it was initially feared that the captain's wife was amongst those lost until it was learned that she had left the ship at Sunderland.

In the following year the Aberdeen schooner *Blossom* with a cargo of quicklime was lost in almost identical circumstances to that of the *Marthas* over fifty years previously. She had sailed from Sunderland at the end of March, with a crew of three, bound for Aberdeen. Off Shields the crew abandoned ship briefly when smoke was seen coming from the deck before reboarding the vessel and putting into port where the fire extinguished itself. In order to make a faster passage as she was obviouly leaky, she left Shields in tow of the tug *America*. All went well until the afternoon of 6 April, by which time they were off Stonehaven, when smoke was seen issuing from the deck where the previous fire had burned a hole. In an effort to smother the fire the captain spread a sail over the burning planking. This promptly caught alight and the flames spread rapidly with the schooner's hull starting to break up as the cargo of lime swelled when it came in contact with water flowing in through a leak. As it was obvious that nothing could be done to save her the crew jumped into the small boat which was being towed astern. A few moments later the schooner's deck burst upwards and the hull disintegrated under the huge pressure of the swelling cargo. There was just sufficient time for the tug's crew to cast off the tow rope before the *Blossom* sank with a rush. Fortunately the weather was reasonably calm and the schooner's crew were soon picked up by the tug and landed at Aberdeen. As an interesting footnote a schooner of the same name and also belonging to Aberdeen had grounded on Cruden Scaurs in the previous February. The crew had been taken off by the Port Erroll lifeboat and the schooner refloated a few days later. If she was the same one then it is clear that she had been badly strained and prone to leaking, the last thing that would be wanted for a vessel carrying a cargo of lime.

The casualties suffered in the storm of March 1881 were appalling by present day standards but mercifully not on the same scale as previous disasters. At least sixteen vessels were wrecked with the loss of over seventy lives on the north-east coast between 4-6 March and this takes no account of the huge amount of unidentified wreckage that also came ashore. As with all of the most dangerous storms the wind blew from the south-east and was accompanied by very heavy falls of snow which blocked roads and railways with huge drifts up to twenty feet deep, bringing life to a complete halt. The casualties positively identified are listed in Appendix 3. There was a complete breakdown in communications and with several vessels driving ashore more or less simultaneously in the same locality contemporary reports are at times, and quite understandably, confused and ambiguous.

The Peterhead registered schooner *Flower of Buchan* was one of the first casualties. She was sighted off Wick at midday on 5 March steering erratically through the breakers in the direction of Noss Head with her sails in tatters and and flying a flag of distress from the foremast head. She brought up under the lee of Castle Sinclair and dropped anchor. As it was obvious that her position was extremely precarious the Board of Trade Rocket Apparatus stationed at Wick was mustered. Some carters' horses were requisitioned when those ordered did not arrive. By the time the rocket cart reached the Ackergill shore the schooner had dragged her anchors and was riding just out of range off the lifeboat slip . The captain finally slipped both anchors, hoisted a staysail and steered for the shore. The schooner being in ballast and therefore light, drove well up the beach and came to rest broadside-on to the shore. The first rocket fired fell short but the second passed through the rigging and the crew of five were quickly brought to land. The master, Captain Alexander Collie, reported that he had sailed from Peterhead on 2 March bound for Sunderland to load a cargo of lime. When they were between the Bell Rock and the Isle of May the weather had deteriorated, the wind coming away from south-south-east and rising rapidly to a severe gale. Unable to carry any canvas which would have helped keep the schooner to windward the captain was forced to run before the weather until the Caithness coast was sighted. In the end with his anchors dragging Captain Collie had little option but to run the schooner ashore. Once on dry land the crew were taken to Ackergill Tower 'where their comforts were attended to' by the proprietor, Mr Duff Dunbar.

By far the largest vessel lost was the 1,247 ton register full-rigged ship *Ben Rhydding* of Liverpool, which stranded on the beach north of the River Don about six hundred yards off Eigie Links. As she proved to be outside the range of the rocket apparatus the Newburgh lifeboat was brought overland but in spite of two attempts it proved impossible to get near the ship because of the huge surf. With the wreck being swept clean by the seas the survivors took refuge in the rigging until about four o'clock that afternoon when the masts went over the side and they were all flung into the surf. None of the crew reached the shore alive but the following day the body of her master Captain John M'Gill was washed up on the beach and identified by papers found in his pockets. By now the *Ben Rhydding* had broken up completely and her cargo of bales of jute from Calcutta was coming ashore along the beach for a mile or more.

At about the same time as the *Ben Rhydding* struck, a dismasted brig driving before the storm was sighted about a mile off Boddam. From her condition it was obvious that she required immediate assistance and the rocket apparatus was called out. In the terrible gale which was accompanied by hail and sleet it proved impossible to get the horses to drag the cart through the huge drifts and in the end it was hauled to the shore by a large number of men. By the time it arrived the brig had disappeared along with her crew, having gone to pieces on the Skerry Rock off the South Bay at Peterhead. Wreckage soon started coming ashore and included in it were the log-book and ship's articles. They identified her as the *Why Not* of Bridport, carrying a crew of six and bound from the Firth of Forth for France with a cargo of coal.

Apart from the larger vessels the small fishing communities along the Buchan coast suffered serious losses. The fishermen petitioned the Hydrographer of the Navy for the construction of a harbour of refuge on the north-east coast. This eventually led to the building of such a harbour at Peterhead by convict labour. (As an interesting footnote twenty-eight of the thirty-seven fishermen from Old Slains who signed the petition had the surname Phillips; survivors perhaps of the *Santa Catarina* who settled locally and took their name from King Philip of Spain?).

Exactly two years later another full-rigged ship, the 1,945 ton gross *Dunstaffnage* of Liverpool was lost with all hands at Findon Ness early in the morning of 17 March. The weather had been appalling with storm force north-easterly winds accompanied with heavy falls of snow causing severe disruption to travel on land and terrible conditions at sea. Having discharged a cargo of jute from Calcutta at Dundee the

Dunstaffnage, in ballast and under the command of Captain Charles Millburn, had cleared the Tay estuary the previous day in tow of the tug *Recovery* bound for Liverpool. She was manned by a crew of runners and also carried the captain's wife and young daughter as passengers. By midnight the two vessels were about twelve miles south-east of Girdle Ness and the weather had deteriorated with the wind rising to storm force. In these conditions the tug and ship made practically no progress until about two o'clock in the morning when the towing hook on the tug carried away along with the hawser. As there was no chance of recovering the tow in the storm the tug steamed southwards before the weather and as she passed the ship her crew could be seen setting sail.

Exactly what happened to the *Dunstaffnage* after that will never be known but by daylight the inhabitants of the small fishing communities in the vicinity of Findon Ness discovered huge quantities of debris coming ashore. There were fragments of cabin furnishings, clothing, parts of a ship's boat, torn pieces of sail, blankets and, as a final confirmation of the disaster a buoy carrying the ship's name. There was no sign of the vessel or any survivors and in a thorough search of the immediate coastline several bodies, all terribly mutilated, were recovered. To add to the tragedy, the captain's son serving as an apprentice, was amongst the twenty-three persons lost. From the distribution of the wreckage it was presumed that the ship had struck Findon Ness before breaking up and slipping back into deep water.

Almost simultaneously with the disaster at Findon Ness another drama was being played out in the howling darkness and storm-tossed waves of the South Bay, Peterhead. The wooden-hulled steam whaler *Mazinthien* of Dundee bound for the Davis Straits had anchored the previous morning through stress of weather. There was a considerable improvement in the conditions later that day which gave no hint of the approaching storm but at dusk a second anchor was dropped as a precaution. By midnight the wind had increased to a north-easterly storm with heavy falls of snow. A huge wave struck the whaler carrying away the hatch covers and flooding the crew's berths. At two o'clock in the morning the anchors started to drag in the storm force winds in spite of the fact that Captain Souter had ordered

4 The crew of the steam whaler *Mazinthien* of Dundee being brought ashore by breeches-buoy on 17 March 1883 at South Bay, Peterhead. (Peterhead Arbuthnot Museum).

the engines to half-speed ahead. As they drifted towards the shore the crew let off distress flares and the Peterhead rocket apparatus was called out.

Conditions were truly appalling and the greatest difficulty was experienced in firing a line to the whaler which by this time had grounded on rocks about five hundred yards offshore. In several attempts the line either missed or parted when it fouled on rocks. Apart from that, the rocket apparatus and some of the brigade were almost washed away on three occasions by enormous waves. At the sixth attempt a rocket struck the whaler amidships and passed clean through the bulwark to the loud cheers of those on board. Infuriatingly, once the hawser had been pulled aboard and secured the lines again fouled on rocks and in the end one of the crew dragged himself ashore hand over hand in an improvised cradle pulling a line behind him. It took well over two hours to bring the crew of twenty-nine men ashore with the last man landing at eleven o'clock. By this time the weather had moderated considerably and later in the afternoon boats went out to salvage the crew's effects and some of the ship's gear. By the following day she had started to break up with one hole in the hull sufficiently large to admit a horse and cart.

Although steamships could ride out all but the severest weather, in times of poor visibility masters were still forced to rely on dead reckoning to establish their positions. In the case of the steamer *Gerona* of Dundee, her master appears to have made insufficient allowance for the strength of the tides off Duncansby Head. She had run ashore on the north side of Freswick Bay below Skirza Head in poor visibility at about four o'clock in the morning of 28 October 1892 while bound from South Shields to Montreal with a general cargo and ten passengers. Both the lights on Noss Head and the Pentland Skerries were invisible in the heavy drizzle which accompanied the strong easterly wind. The steamer grounded on a ledge of rock about one hundred yards from the shore with her bow and midship section held fast and the stern floating clear in deep water. Although the rocket brigade were quickly on the scene, attempts to fire a line aboard failed and in the end one was floated ashore secured to a buoy. The landward end of the main hawser was secured round a convenient house and a cradle improvised from a four cran fish basket. In this way the ten passengers, nine of whom belonged to

5 Salvage operations on the Dundee steamer *Gerona* ashore Skirza Head, Caithness, 28 October 1892; cargo being transferred ashore by ropeway. The steamer was refloated the following month. (From the Johnston Collection by permission of the Wick Society).

the Southern family emigrating to Toronto, were brought ashore
with their luggage.

Later that day at high water an attempt by several steam
trawlers to refloat the stranded steamer failed when the hawsers
parted. By now she had started to leak with up to eight feet of
water in some compartments and it was obvious that the ship
would have to be lightened if there was any chance of her being
towed off. The crew started to discharge the bunker coal over the
side and the salvage steamer *Clyde* was dispatched from Leith
with divers and pumps. The weather remained unsettled,
delaying operations somewhat but by the following week most
of the cargo which consisted of cement, nitrate of soda, bricks
and pig-iron was either thrown over the side or in the case of the
iron loaded into boats and taken ashore. On 3 November the
weather worsened and to prevent the ship from pounding in the
heavy swell the after hold was flooded by cutting a small hole in
the hull but she sustained further damage two days later in
freshening winds. Another squad of men was sent from Wick to
discharge more of the cargo so that the new leaks could be
located and plugged. Finally, at midnight on 6 November the
combined efforts of two tugs, a steam trawler and a kedge
anchor connected by a six inch hawser to the steamer's winch
dragged the *Gerona* off the ledge into deep water. In spite of the
extra pumping capacity the water started to gain and the steamer
had to be beached on the sands below Freswick House. Divers
discovered a large hole midships, well below the water-line which
required extensive patching before she was sufficently seaworthy
to be towed south for repairs. It was also discovered that the
engines had been damaged and the propellor shaft and stern post
broken. Once the worst of the leaks had been plugged the
steamer was towed to the Cromarty Firth and from thence to
Dundee for major repairs.

The coastline between Aberdeen and Stonehaven consists of
rugged cliffs and although steep-to, is fringed by rocky ledges on
which many well found ships have come to grief. As an
additional hazard the coast could at times be shrouded by 'haar'
or coastal fog which reduced visibility to virtually nil. The
Aberdeen registered steamer *Countess of Aberdeen* under the
command of Captain Joss had sailed from Hull on her last
voyage early on the morning of 15 April 1894 bound for

Aberdeen with twelve passengers and a general cargo which included four horses carried on deck. At first conditions were excellent with the weather fine and the sea calm, so that the steamer had a splendid passage until she approached the Kincardine coast later that evening. A mist began to form which completely enveloped the shore reducing the visibility to a few yards. Unknown to the captain the steamer had been set inshore by the flood tide and by ten o'clock was sufficently close to the land for the coastguards at Cove to hear the beat of her propellor in the still conditions. Realising that the ship was too close to land they fired a signal gun several times to warn her that she was standing into danger. Those on the bridge apparently heard nothing and, in what the *Aberdeen Journal* called 'an accident of a serious nature' the *Countess* ran hard on the rocks at the north side of Cove Bay. She immediately settled down, listing to starboard, remaining fast in spite of the engines being put full astern.

Captain Joss, realising that there was little chance of her being refloated under her own power, gave the order to abandon ship. There were considerable problems with the lifeboat which had jammed in the davits owing to the list and once launched, it promptly capsized before righting and drifting round the stern. At this point the steamer lurched heavily throwing one of the female passengers and her child into the water. Her husband immediately jumped in and pulled both of them to safety. Although she was not missed till a few minutes later, it would appear that the stewardess, a Miss Gordon, also fell in the water at this time and drowned unseen. Fishermen and coastguards having heard the noise of the steamer running on the rocks immediately rowed out to help in the rescue. With the weather remaining calm the passengers were soon transferred ashore and taken to the Cove Hotel for shelter. Meanwhile, Captain Joss organised a search on board the stranded steamer for the missing stewardess but no sign of her could be found. After two hours they gave up and made for the shore. Shortly afterwards a fire broke out in the stern section, probably due to one of the paraffin lamps having overturned in the stranding, and burned unchecked until there was nothing left to feed the flames. On the following morning smoke was seen coming from the forecastle and flames were soon bursting through the decks to burn unchecked. The day after, a heavy ground swell completed the destruction and the steamer broke up and sank. A considerable amount of cargo and baggage came ashore including several cases of oranges which were salvaged and promptly consumed by the Cove 'loons'.

Later the same year the Sunderland registered steamer *Chicago* belonging to the Neptune Steam Navigation Company ran on the rocks of the Ward of Cruden immediately below Slains Castle at full speed. Described as a 'splendid schooner rigged vessel, equipped with the most approved appliances', she had sailed from her home port on 9 October bound for Baltimore with 130 tons of general cargo. Having safely rounded Cruden Skares shortly after midnight in poor visibility and a stiff southerly wind, the second officer who was on watch, saw an unidentified light ahead and immediately called the captain. As they were to shortly to find out the ship was right under the Ward and in spite of the engines being full astern she struck the rocks. So violent was the impact that a large block of granite was broken clean off, the steamer's three forward compartments holed and the ship stuck fast on an underwater ledge. In fact she was so close to the shore that a coachman at Slains Castle heard her striking the rocks and warned the nearby coastguard station. Although the engines were run full astern for two hours there was not the slightest chance of the steamer being refloated. In the end the crew were taken off by the local Rocket Brigade watched by a large audience who had forsaken a servants' ball being held at the castle.

In spite of the completion of rail links to Caithness the ports of Wick and Scrabster were served up to the Second World War by steamers from Aberdeen which carried freight and passengers on a regular schedule with connections to the Northern Isles. They were owned by the North of Scotland, Orkney and Shetland Steam Navigation Company, usually known as 'The North Boats' or 'North of Scotland', and in spite of the sometimes severe weather and difficult conditions encountered, had an enviable safety record. Wick, with its narrow and exposed entrance was the scene of the stranding and eventual salvage of one of the 'North Boats' steamers in February 1895. The *St Clair*, northbound from Aberdeen, having discharged some passengers and cargo was leaving the port early in the

6 The 'North of Scotland' steamer *St Clair* being pounded by waves at the back of the North Pier, Wick, having gone ashore on 30 January 1895 while leaving port, refloated the following March. (Aberdeen City Arts Department, Art Gallery and Museums).

morning of 30 January. As she cleared the South Pier in a fresh south-easterly wind which had raised a heavy swell she took the ground in the trough of a wave. With her way checked, the bow fell away to the westward and the steamer drove ashore on rocks about fifty yards off the North Pier. The rocket apparatus and lifeboat were immediately called out on a bitterly cold morning there, having been heavy falls of snow earlier in the month. A line was soon fired aboard and the stewardess, a Miss Allan, was the first person saved barely an hour after the initial call-out. With the Wick lifeboat lying off all five passengers and thirty-two crew were pulled ashore, Captain Nisbet being the last man to leave. By high water that afternoon the swell was sweepng right over the stranded steamer and her position looked bleak.

In spite of this, salvage equipment was dispatched from Leith with Mr Armit of the East Coast Salvage Association, who had previously salvaged the *Gerona*, in charge. Operations were severely delayed by blizzards, and low temperatures caused compressed air lines to freeze up. The hull, holed in the engine room and forward, had to be patched by divers and all cargo discharged. It was not until a month after first running ashore that the ship started to come alive. By 26 February she had been hauled some forty feet astern by a tug and even further the following week. She was finally refloated on 13 March and came off the rocks with such a rush that her stern collided with the South Pier stoving in one of the plates. As it was a half-holiday in Wick, a large number of people had gathered to watch operations and they helped tow the vessel to the North Pier. To complete the carnival atmosphere the *St Clair* was dressed over all with bunting and boarded by large numbers of spectators. After further patching work she was finally towed to Aberdeen in April for repairs.

Later that month the Norwegian brig *Caledonia* with a cargo of pit props for Troon was discovered by the steam trawler *Sheldrake* of North Shields drifting derelict about sixty miles north east of Peterhead. The crew were taken off and reported that they had been buffeted by heavy weather for three weeks which caused the brig to spring a leak and only the cargo of pit props had saved her from sinking. As it seemed likely that she would continue to float the *Sheldrake* took her in tow and arrived safely in Wick Bay. From a contemporary photograph it

7 The derelict Norwegian brig *Caledonia* in Wick Bay, April 1895, decks awash and barely afloat. (From the Johnston Collection by permission of the Wick Society).

seems incredible that the brig had in fact remained afloat. She lies with decks awash, the fore-top mast hangs over the side, her main mast has been sprung and the panels of the bulwarks have been completely swept away, altogether a sorry, battered sight.

The Neptune Steam Navigation Company could have been forgiven for thinking that the coast of North East Scotland carried some sort of jinx for them when another of their ships, the *Ohio*, ran ashore in thick fog on the Caithness coast at Auckengill early on the morning on 28 May 1897. She had been bound from Rotterdam with a part cargo of sugar, cement, toys and spirits. The master's wife and child were sent ashore and lodged locally when the swell increased and the steamer was driven broadside to the shore. An attempt by the steam liner *Fleetwing* and the Kirkwall steamer *Express* to tow the stranded vessel off failed and Mr Armit of the East Coast Salvage Association was summoned from Leith. Fortunately, she had gone ashore at low water but in a freshening easterly wind the hull pounded on the rocky shore and she started to leak badly with the rudder carrying away. The coal bunkers were jettisoned and most of the cargo was discharged although ten casks of gin had their ends stove in and the contents run into the sea. Steam pumps were transferred aboard but with only small neap tides she still remained fast in spite of the efforts of no less than four tugs trying to pull her off. It was not until 12 June that larger tides provided sufficient water for the steamer to be refloated and then beached in Sinclair's Bay for further patching. By the following week she was safely berthed in Aberdeen graving dock for further temporary repairs.

9

'A Veritable Trap for Shipping'

By the beginning of the twentieth century sailing vessels were becoming a memory of the past with steam power completely dominating the world's merchant fleets. However, some owners, particularly those in Scandinavia, still maintained a small number of sailing vessels of substantial size which continued in service until the outbreak of the Second World War. The Swedish barque *Hans* of Landskrona bound from Florida with a cargo of rosin for Granton had been disabled in a severe north-westerly gale while passing through the Pentland Firth in early May 1900. With the rudder, wheel and sails carried away she was rendered completely unmanageable and Captain Lenander hoisted distress signals. The Scrabster lifeboat was called out but discovered that the master was in fact signalling for a tug or steamer to take him in tow and her assistance was declined. By now the Longhope lifeboat had put to sea while the one at Huna had also been called out but sustained damage in the launching. With the two boats in pursuit the barque safely rounded Duncansby Head where her crew abandoned ship once she started to leak. They were picked by a steam trawler which tried unsuccessfully to take the *Hans* in tow and she finally drifted away with the distress signals still flying. With the crew now safe both lifeboats made for Wick where, later that day, the barque was sighted off the port drifting towards the land. The Wick lifeboat was then launched but by that time the *Hans* had drifted ashore stern first at the Broadhaven just north of the harbour entrance. On that rocky section of coast there could be no hope of salvage and the wreck was sold later that month for £110.

The rocks of Rattray Head continued to cause severe losses

8 The Swedish barque *Hans*, 1,229 tons gross, ashore at Broadhaven, Wick, having been abandoned off Duncansby Head, 1 May 1900. The windmill-like device between the main and mizzen masts provided power for the ship's pumps indicating that she was old and leaky. (From the Johnston Collection by permission of the Wick Society).

particularly in times of poor visibility. In the early autumn of 1902 the 'North of Scotland' steamer *St Giles* south bound from Lerwick, ran ashore in dense fog on the Briggs about a quarter mile north of the lighthouse. She had sailed on the evening of 27 September with seventy passengers and a quantity of livestock. Fog was encountered off the Moray Firth and speed reduced according to Board of Trade regulations. In spite of the poor visibility Captain Williamson felt sufficiently certain of the ship's position to go below for the first breakfast sitting. He had just returned on deck and the second party served with the fish course when according to one passenger, a native of the Faroes splendidly named Captain Napolean Anderson, the steamer struck the Briggs throwing everything off the saloon tables and the passengers were sent flying in all directions. Not surprisingly there was something of a panic initially, but order was soon restored and stewards started to issue lifejackets. With a fair swell running the steamer rolled heavily on the rocks but the lifeboats were safely launched and the passengers landed on the beach to be looked after by the inhabitants of Botany. As it was clear that there was no chance of the steamer being refloated all of the livestock was dropped over the side and allowed to swim to the land with the mail and most of the freight ferried ashore by boat. At low water, the steamer with only her bow and stern resting firmly on the rocks, sagged badly and she soon broke her back.

In November of the following year the 268 ton iron brigantine *Astrea* of Christiansund struck the outermost point of The Skares south of Cruden Bay and became a total loss. She had been bound for Fraserburgh with a cargo of barrel staves when a southerly gale sprang up and visibility reduced by a thick haze. The brigantine struck before dawn on 14 November and as she filled rapidly her crew had to take to the rigging. They were sighted an hour later by a fisherman at Whinnyfold and as there was no chance of any of the local boats putting off in the heavy surf the Port Erroll rocket brigade was called out. In spite of repeated attempts it proved impossible to fire a line aboard the brigantine which was lying too far offshore. By this time the wretched crew were suffering severely from repeated soakings and the effects of cold with the ship's boy having to be lashed to the mast as he was completely unable to hold on to the rigging.

Finally, in answer to a telegram the Peterhead lifeboat was towed south by a tug and after spending over five hours stranded in the rigging the *Astrea*'s crew of eight were rescued.

Considering the extremely large number of ships which passed the coasts of North East Scotland at the beginning of the twentieth century collisions were remarkably infrequent. In the case of the steamers *James Hall* and *Luddick* which collided off Aberdeen Beach on 23 February 1904 the accident was due quite simply to poor seamanship. Both vessels had been making for the harbour in clear weather and although dark the visibility was good. The *James Hall* crossed the *Luddick*'s bow and was struck and badly holed on the port quarter. As she immediately began to settle the captain ordered the crew to abandon ship leaving her head to land and the engines running so that she eventually ran ashore just north of the Bathing Station. Although badly damaged about the stem and leaking heavily the *Luddick* picked up the *James Hall*'s crew and managed to limp into Aberdeen. On the following day all the Aberdeen Corporation trams on the beach route carried notices 'To & From the Stranded Steamer', whoever managed the organisation having an extremely well developed sense of business.

Later that year the little coastal steamer *Nar* of Glasgow foundered in a north-north-easterly storm off Speymouth with the loss of her crew of nine men. She had been bound for Burghead with a cargo of coal and having been overtaken by the storm anchored off to ride it out. Shortly after midnight on 14 December a coastguard on duty at Kingston saw signals of distress and the rocket apparatus was summoned. They fired several star rockets but as there was no answer the brigade betook themselves to shelter to wait for daylight. A search of the beach at dawn recovered four bodies, two ship's boats, a considerable quantity of wreckage and a lifebuoy carrying the words *Nar* Glasgow. There was no sign of the steamer which was only located the following week when the foremast, still attached to the hull, was discovered floating about a mile offshore in about six fathoms of water. In that position and with the shallow gently shelving bottom, any northerly gales would have produced extremely heavy breaking seas quite capable of causing a steamer like the *Nar* to founder.

With the rise of steam power at sea the fishing industry at

9 The wreck of the Aberdeen steamer *James Hall* which drifted ashore at Aberdeen Beach on 23 February 1904 after colliding with the Luddick. (Aberdeen City Arts Department, Art Gallery and Museums).

Aberdeen underwent a massive expansion and by the early 1900s the city was by far the largest fishing port in Scotland. The need to conserve stocks was recognised early on and the Scottish Fishery Board maintained a research station at Aberdeen. At the end of 1905 the local steam trawler *Star of Hope* had been chartered by the Board to carry out investigation work in Aberdeen Bay under the supervision of one of the Board's scientists, Mr John Burgoyne. Having trawled in the bay till darkness fell she hauled her nets intending to lie off till day break. For unexplained reasons and with the skipper having just left the bridge she ran onto rocks about one mile north of the River Ythan between one and two o'clock the following morning. With their vessel badly holed and filling fast the crew took refuge on top of the galley while Burgoyne climbed into the foremast rigging. In spite of burning flares for over four hours they failed to attract any attention ashore and all of the men suffered severely from the cold and wet. By daybreak, Burgoyne completely numbed by the cold, had lost his grip on the rigging and fallen into the sea. Even worse, the unfortunate chief engineer had to watch helplessly as both his sons died, one swept away by a wave and the other succumbing to exposure. It was not until ten o'clock that morning that the wreck was spotted and the alarm raised ashore. Even then there were more inexplicable delays and it was after midday before the rocket apparatus arrived on the scene. With the wrecked trawler lying less than a hundred yards offshore a line was easily got aboard and the six survivors quickly brought to safety.

Just over two months later at the end of January 1906 the coastal steamer *Kenilworth* struck rocks off Cove while bound for Aberdeen with a cargo of coal. With his steamer badly holed Captain Scorgie made for Aberdeen at full speed but with the water gaining rapidly had to run her ashore at Burnbanks Haven, Altens, before she sank. The steamer had been seen in difficulties by coastguards at Cove and the rocket apparatus was immediately dispatched northwards in pursuit. By the time they arrived at Burnbanks the crew had already abandoned ship and there was no one aboard when a line was fired across the stranded steamer's bows. The crew had in fact left the ship with the intention of rowing to Aberdeen but decided to land at Nigg Bay because of the heavy seas running on the bar. They set off

10 The collier *Kenilworth* partly submerged off Burnbanks, Cove, south of Aberdeen, 30 January 1906. (Aberdeen City Arts Department, Libraries).

on foot for town unaware that a tug dispatched to pick them up at sea, had found nothing and a full scale search was now under way. It was only called off when they finally turned up safe if somewhat footsore at the company's offices later that evening.

In January 1912 the coast of North East Scotland was struck by a terrible south-easterly storm which lasted for over a week. Three steamers were driven ashore between Aberdeen and Peterhead with the loss of sixty-eight lives. In the prolonged onshore winds huge seas were raised along the coast and with the port of Aberdeen more or less impassable to shipping, vessels were forced to lie off or run for shelter before the weather. The first casualty was the 406 ton *Argosy* which had sailed from London with a cargo of cement for her home port of Aberdeen. By the time she arrived off the harbour entrance early on the morning of 17 January the storm was at its height and there was no chance of crossing the bar until high water later that morning. When Captain Paterson did finally try to run for the entrance shortly before midday the steering gear broke down and the steamer, swept by huge seas, was carried northwards towards the beach. The engine room and bunkers were rapidly flooded with the engineers and firemen working frantically to maintain steam. On deck, the bridge and wheelhouse had been severely damaged with everything moveable swept away. By the time the *Argosy* drove ashore just north of the Bathing Station a large crowd had gathered and they helped drag the lifeboat along the beach. In spite of the huge surf and by brilliant seamanship the lifeboatmen managed to row alongside the steamer which was rolling heavily and take off all the crew to the loud cheers of the crowd. Large numbers of them then waded into the sea to help drag the lifeboat ashore. The transport authorities had obligingly laid on a special tram service to the beach which had helped to swell the crowd but cars had some difficulty in reaching their destination as the rails kept filling with wind-blown sand. Once on dry land the steamer's crew were taken to the nearby Bathing Station where they were given hot baths and a further warming in the furnace room. Although badly battered the *Argosy* was discharged and eventually refloated.

An hour after the *Argosy* went ashore an unidentified steamer, listing heavily and flying distress signals, foundered

11 The steamer *Argosy* being pounded by heavy surf after being driven ashore on Aberdeen Beach on 17 January 1912. (Aberdeen City Arts Department, Art Gallery and Museums).

off Whinnyfold just south of Port Erroll. It was not until the following day that she was positively identified as the Aberdeen collier *Frederick Snowden* when a name board was washed ashore near Peterhead. Although an old vessel, she had been built at Middlesborough in 1866, her master, Captain John Auld, was an extremely experienced seaman and she had just completed her annual Board of Trade survey. There were no survivors from the crew of thirteen and the reasons for her loss remained something of a mystery. By a bitter irony one of those drowned included a stoker, Henry Mitchell, who had been a noted lifeguard at Aberdeen Beach saving over a hundred lives.

There was an even greater tragedy at sunrise the following day. A large steamer, lying dead in the water and firing distress flares, was seen off Cruden Bay by lookouts at Port Erroll Coastguard Station. She was drifting before the storm towards the coast and as it was obvious that she would come ashore the local rocket brigade was called out. They followed the steamer along the coast as she drifted northwards towards the terrible granite cliffs and ledges at North Haven. At first it was hoped that she would drive right into the Haven with a fair chance of some of the crew being rescued. In the event she struck the Tempion, a huge bulwark-like rock lying at the Haven entrance and immediately started to break up. The rocket brigade fired two lines aboard the stricken steamer but with the deck being swept by huge waves there was no chance for anyone to secure the whips. Horrified spectators could only watch helplessly as the crew were washed away and disappeared in the boiling surf. There seemed little left to do but recover any bodies which came ashore and take them to the little Mission Hall which had been pressed into service as a temporary mortuary.

Incredibly four men reached the shore alive through the surf and floating wreckage. They included the captain who identified the steamer as the *Wistow Hall* of Liverpool bound from the Tyne to Glasgow in ballast with a crew of fourteen Europeans and forty-three Lascars. She had been completely disabled off the Longstone Lighthouse by the storm with the funnel being swept away and the stokehold flooded. Two Lascars had been killed and the captain and mate injured. Thereafter, with the engines dead she had drifted northwards before the storm to drive ashore at North Haven. All the bodies of those lost were buried at St James Church, Cruden Bay and their grave marked with a simple stone of pink Peterhead granite.

Initially it was thought that there had been another casualty. In the early hours of the 18th, the lights of a vessel driving north before the storm had been seen off Rattray Head only to disappear abruptly. When the weather moderated a few days later, fishermen discovered a mast floating in the water and attached to some wreckage on the seabed. In fact, it was identified as coming from the *Frederick Snowden*.

A year later there was further tragic loss of life when a Danish steamer was driven ashore at Girdle Ness in a south-easterly storm. The *G. Koch* of Odense, bound for Burntisland in water ballast and with a deck cargo of pit props encountered severe weather in the North Sea. Having run low on coal the crew had been forced to burn part of the cargo to maintain steam but were driven northwards before the storm and struck the rocks below Girdle Ness Lighthouse shortly after midnight on 12 January. She had been seen by coastguards at Cove who called out the rocket apparatus and they reached the scene shortly afterwards. Because of the extremely dangerous position the brigades from Torry and Donmouth were also called out in order to try to rescue the crew as quickly as possible. In spite of this lines repeatedly fouled on floating wreckage and some of the crew, in a fatal attempt to reach safety, tried to haul themselves hand-over-hand along one of the hawsers. Although some reached the shore seven men either fell off through exhaustion or were washed away by the surf. At daylight some survivors were spotted aboard the wreck and with the tide ebbing a line was passed aboard which allowed a breeches buoy to be hauled out and the eleven remaining survivors to be pulled ashore.

In June of the following year with the east coast of Scotland shrouded in thick fog two steamers were totally wrecked on the coast of Caithness. They were the *Thyra* of Tonsberg bound for New York, ashore at the Stacks of Duncansby on 11 June and the *St Nicholas* belonging to the 'North Boats' which stranded on the Proudfoot Rocks six days later while trying to enter Wick. The weather remained calm and at first there were hopes that the *Thyra* could be patched and refloated but she developed serious leaks and all efforts had to be concentrated on salvaging the cargo which included bagging, burlap, skins, school bags,

12 The stern section of the Danish steamer *G. Koch* wrecked on Girdle Ness 12 January 1913 with the loss of seven of her crew. (Aberdeen City Arts Department, Art Gallery and Museums).

lime juice, spirits, tea, pianos, hides, star antimony and copper matte. In the case of the *St Nicholas* she had sailed from Scrabster to load a consignment of herring at Wick for Leith. Although she ran onto a sloping ledge she was not holed but slipped off and sank in deep water about six hours later. Some of her cargo of sheep and 'cattle beasts' swam ashore with a pilot boat towing one bullock into the harbour. Salvage work on both wrecks was abruptly suspended in August when Europe went mad and the terrible slaughter of the First World War commenced.

Initial casualties of the war were in fact caused by all coastal lights being extinguished and shipping was in more danger of running ashore at night than in being sunk by enemy action. The *Aberdeen Daily Journal* aptly described Rattray Head as 'a veritable trap for shipping' when two Swedish steamers ran ashore there at the end of October 1914 within two days of one another. The *Blanka* of Oscarshamn with a cargo of timber for Hull had run ashore at three o'clock on 29 October about two miles north of Rattray Head Lighthouse. In spite of having struck at low water it proved impossible to refloat the steamer and the crew were taken off by the Peterhead lifeboat. With a full north-east gale blowing and all coastal lights extinguished her master reported that he had great difficulty in establishing his position.

Two days later the *Torgrim* of Landkrona, timber laden for Grangemouth, went ashore in identical circumstances close to the *Blanka*. The Peterhead lifeboat was again called out in the continuing gale but had to put back almost immediately with engine trouble so the rowing lifeboat was launched and towed to Rattray Head by a trawler. While off the casualty the lifeboat was completely swamped and had to be run ashore before any of the crew could be taken off. By now both the Peterhead and Rattray rocket brigades were in attendance but it proved impossible to fire a line to the steamer. In the end a rope lashed to a plank was thrown overboard and this fouled a rocket line which finally allowed the breeches buoy to be pulled aboard. The crew of nineteen which included two women, all by now soaked, frozen and exhausted were brought ashore to the cheers of the onlookers.

At the beginning of February 1915 the coast was struck by a

particularly severe easterly gale in which three ships were driven ashore in the vicinity of Peterhead, namely the destroyer HMS *Erne* at Rattray Head, the Admiralty trawler *Daniel Stroud* and the Hull steamer *Salvor No. 1*. So far as can be gathered there was no loss of life with either of the naval vessels but only one of the crew from the salvage ship was saved. She had been anchored in the South Bay but while shifting her anchorage for more sheltered moorings had capsized and drifted ashore below the brickworks immediately south of the town. The cook was trapped below deck and was only spotted when his hand was seen waving from one of the portholes of the upturned hull. It was through the gallant efforts of a local boilermaker, Francis M'Robbie, that he was cut free. Having dragged oxy-acetylene cutting equipment over the rocks M'Robbie stood for almost an hour up to his neck in water until a hole had been made in the hull and the trapped cook pulled to safety.

The first civilian vessel to be lost through enemy action was the three-masted topsail schooner *Sunbeam* of Chester commanded by Captain William Moodie. On 4 July 1915 she was intercepted off the Caithness coast by a German submarine whilst on a voyage to Westray with a cargo of coal. Her crew were given five minutes to abandon ship in their small boat before the schooner was sunk by gunfire from the submarine. They were later picked up by an Admiralty trawler and landed at Wick. Soon afterwards Captain Moodie joined a 'Q' ship and was later awarded the D.S.C. for his part in the sinking of a German submarine.

The 647 ton barque *Teutonic* of Langesund was the last sailing vessel of substantial size to be wrecked on the coast of North East Scotland when she went to pieces on the Findon Rocks in the early hours of 29 October. She had been bound for Leith with a cargo of pit props and had reached the Firth of Forth when the wind rapidly increased to a south-east storm. It proved impossible to remain in the Firth and with the cargo being swept overboard the master tried to stand out to sea in the worsening conditions. However she then sprang a leak and with five feet of water in the waist of the ship the captain ordered the crew to jettison all of the remaining deck cargo. It proved impossible to set any sails and shortly after midnight the barque drifted amongst the rocks of Findon Ness where she broke in two in a matter of minutes. The stern section remained intact to be driven into the creek at Arnot Boo where the survivors scrambled ashore across a floating mass of pit props. Five of the crew were lost, either drowned in the huge seas or crushed by the floating cargo.

At the end of the year the relative peace of the Grand Fleet base at Invergordon was shattered by a massive explosion when the armoured cruiser HMS *Natal* blew up and sank at her moorings in the Cromarty Firth. As it was Hogmanay a party of thirteen civilians which included several children were aboard being entertained with a film show in the wardroom. They were lost together with some 350 officers and men and only 283 survivors were picked up from the waters of the Firth with some of them dying later. The explosion was almost certainly caused by the detonation of unstable cordite in one of the stern mag-azines; there being no conclusive evidence to support subsequent claims that the cruiser had been sunk by a German 'infernal machine'. The wreck, lying on her side with the bilge above water was a major navigational hazard and was sold in 1921 for scrap. Operations proved uneconomic and sections of her hull still lie on the bottom of the Firth about a mile and a half west of Cromarty lighthouse.

In the first half of 1917 the Germans launched a submarine offensive against shipping off the north-east coast with eleven ships being sunk by mine or torpedo between Wick and Tod Head. Because of severe censorship details of the sinkings are extremely sparse but the loss of the minesweeper H.M. Trawler *Pitstruan* seems to be fairly typical. She had been escorting a trawler about two miles south-east of Noss Head when two floating mines were sighted. All hands were mustered on deck and ordered to wear lifejackets with a lookout posted in the bows. Shortly afterwards the trawler exploded a moored mine and sank immediately. The drifter *Lapwing* picked up two survivors, her commander and a trimmer, who were both suffering from shock and burns and landed them at Wick.

Coastal shipping running to fixed schedules was a particular target with the result that the *St Magnus* was attacked and sunk off Peterhead on 12 February 1918. She had been bound from Lerwick for Aberdeen when she was torpedoed without warning by a submarine at about noon. In the calm weather all of the passengers and crew with the exception of one of the engine room staff were able to get away in two of the ship's boats before being picked up by a minesweeper and landed at Peterhead. The German authorities justified their lack of warning when attacking the steamer by claiming that as the *St Magnus* was armed she could therefore classified as a warship.

With the cessation of hostilities casualties declined to peacetime levels as coastal lights were relit and shipping was able to resume pre-war routes. The Copenhagen registered steamer *Kentucky* bound for Boston was an early post-war casualty when she ran aground below Skirza Head on 30 December 1920. As she was hard aground the crew were landed the following day along with twenty-seven bags of mail. After many setbacks due to bad weather which seriously hampered salvage operations the Leith Salvage and Towage Company finally refloated her on 9 March. With the aid of tugs and her own engines she was beached in Wick Bay in order to complete patching work. While being towed to Aberdeen she had to be beached in the Cromarty Firth for further repairs when the water in the after holds started gaining on the pumps. It was not until 30 March that she reached her destination and after lying in the harbour for many months she was finally sold for scrapping in Germany.

There continued to be casualties on the Buchan coast in times of poor visibility. The 5,245 ton Cairn Line steamer *Cairnavon* of Newcastle bound for Montreal with a general cargo ran ashore in dense fog a mile south of Buchan Ness Lighthouse in the early hours of 1 November 1925. In fact the fog was so dense that the lightkeepers were completely unaware of the wreck until the arrival of coasguards searching for the steamer. Wick Radio had in fact picked up the SOS broadcast by the ship but because of the poor visibility it was two hours before the Peterhead rocket brigade could locate her. Meanwhile the situation had become so precarious that the order to abandon ship was given and the crew and one passenger scrambled onto rocks lying under the bow via a rope ladder. The mate and three men, carrying torches to help them find a way in the pitch darkness started to climb the cliff but by this time the coastguards had located the steamer and a cliff ladder was lowered. In an extremely difficult operation they and the forty-five men still at the bottom were brought to safety. There was no chance of salvaging the steamer which broke in two later that day.

By 1925 salvage operations on the scuttled German High Seas Fleet at Scapa Flow were well in hand with the warships raised being towed to the Firth of Forth for breaking up. One of these, the destroyer *G 103*, broke adrift during a squall in the Moray Firth while being towed south by the Aberdeen tug *Audax*. The derelict hulk drifted ashore at Locheilair about a mile west of Rosehearty early in the morning of 25 November. In the heavy seas she quickly broke in two and was discovered by coastguards lying just below highwater mark. Given her light construction and the exposed position she was quickly reduced to a mass of broken plates and frames.

10

Peace and War

In spite of the deepening economic recession in the mid 1920s Aberdeen still continued to be the largest fishing port in Scotland. The price was high and between the two World Wars at least thirty steam trawlers were wrecked on the north-east coast. In the case of the *Ben Torc* of Aberdeen there was fortunately no loss of life in spite of running ashore in an extremely exposed position on Greg Ness just south of Aberdeen. On 6 September 1927 she had been bound for her home port having bunkered in Granton. A stiff south-east wind had raised heavy seas on the coast which was blanketed in thick fog. Shortly before ten o'clock in the evening the trawler ran hard aground with the swell swinging the bow round to face the sea. The siren was sounded continuously in distress and coastguards from the nearby station at Greg Ness were soon on the scene. Having swum a small gully at considerable risk they managed to pass a line aboard to the crew who then decided that they would prefer to be taken off by lifeboat. It was while the six men were jumping aboard her that the skipper George Rose attired in bowler hat fell in the sea and was duly hauled to safety still wearing his head gear.

In the following March fog again caused serious problems with no less than six vessels running ashore. The largest was the Haugesund registered steamer *Echo* which grounded on rocks in Strathlethen Bay, a mile south of Stonehaven, on the evening of 6 March. The master, Captain Gravdal, had thought that his ship was thirty miles out at sea. Because the ship was settling rapidly the crew abandoned ship without making any distress signals and made south completely unaware that Stonehaven lay

13 Hard aground on Aberdeen Beach after being driven ashore on 7 January 1929, the Ellerman Wilson steamer, *Idaho* was only refloated in the following July after a major salvage operation. (Aberdeen City Arts Department, Art Gallery and Museums).

only a mile to the north. Off Tod Head they realised there was no chance of landing on that section of coast and started to row back north. Nine hours after first leaving their ship the crew, by now completely exhausted, arrived back off Strathlethen Bay to be guided ashore by a fisherman.

The Ellerman's steamer *Idaho* bound from Hull to New York via Aberdeen encountered thick fog off the east coast of Scotland at the beginning of January 1929. In spite of the efforts of three tugs she ran aground close to the Beach Ballroom while trying to enter the harbour. As the steamer had stranded on a sandy bottom and suffered no damage the crew remained aboard. On the following day an attempt to tow her off failed when the hawsers kept parting and one tug had to be towed back to port with a rope round her propellor. An attempt to unload the cargo of flour by a 'Blondin' set up on the beach failed so a small fleet of local fishing yawls was chartered to transfer the cargo ashore. The operation proved hazardous with one of the boats capsizing while loading and another being narrowly missed by a sack which fell out of a sling. A fortnight after stranding the steamer's crew were paid off when it became obvious that there was little chance of her being refloated in the near future.

By mid-February some 2,000 tons of cargo had been offloaded and the bunker coal jettisoned but a succession of onshore winds kept driving the ship further up the beach. The jettisoned coal was eagerly recovered from the beach by a small swarm of unoffical salvage operators who fished it up before it could wash away. Another attempt to tow her off at spring tides in the middle of March failed and it seemed likely that the *Idaho* was destined to become a permanent feature of Aberdeen Beach. However as she had suffered little damage the decision was taken to continue salvage operations and these continued throughout the spring and well into summer. By the middle of July tugs had managed to pull the bow round until it pointed seawards and on the 16th the tug *Bulger* with the aid of an exceptionally high tide finally dragged her off into deep water. She floated with a distinct list to port but was towed into Aberdeen for temporary repairs without any problems.

In September of the following year another Ellerman's steamer the *City of Osaka* ran on the rocks north of Collieston

14 The 6,614 ton gross Liverpool steamer *City of Osaka* ashore below granite cliffs just south of Cruden Skares, 25 September 1930. (Aberdeen City Arts Department, Art Gallery and Museums).

in mist and rain while on a voyage from Newcastle to New York with a small cargo of timber. Although her SOS was picked up by Wick Radio and she sounded her siren, visibility was so bad that she was only discovered about a mile south of the Skares of Cruden after a two hour search. The life saving apparatus was directed to the spot and by ten o'clock forty men had been brought ashore with the remainder electing to be taken off by lifeboat. Having returned with their apparatus to Collieston the men were called out again when the steamer radioed for assistance and another line was fired aboard. However, the master refused to land by breeches buoy and all of those remaining on board were taken off by the Peterhead lifeboat. In the following days the stranded steamer was driven further ashore until her bows were awash and the stern clear of the water with no hope of her ever being refloated.

The circumstances of the loss of the Ijmuiden trawler *Noordpool* at Rosehearty in the early hours of 1 March 1931 remain a mystery. Admittedly the weather was abominable with gale force north-north-easterly winds and heavy snow showers but her skipper, Job Gravenmaker, had fished the Moray Firth for twenty-eight years. No distress signals had been seen or heard and the wreck was only discovered at daylight lying on her port side with keel to shore about 500 yards west of Rosehearty Pier. There was no sign of any survivors or bodies when the wreck was searched by Inspector Michie of the local constabulary and a Mr Michie, the local chemist. The ship's clock which was washed ashore had stopped at one minute to five. From her size it was presumed that the trawler had carried a crew of between twelve and fourteen hands. In all ten bodies were recovered from the shore and interred at Kirkton Cemetery in arctic conditions. In spite of this there was a huge procession of mourners over half a mile long which included local dignitaries and the crew of a Dutch trawler berthed at Aberdeen. Later that year Captain Gravenmaker's body was exhumed and taken back to Holland for burial.

Shortly after ten o'clock on the night of 2 December 1931 lookouts at Collieston Coastguard Station observed distress flares off the coast in the vicinity of Broadhaven. With the wind blowing a full south-south easterly gale accompanied by heavy rain the life saving company was summoned by maroon. When

15 After running ashore in early hours of 1 March 1931 the Dutch trawler *Noordpool* lies on the rocks just west of Rosehearty. (Peterhead Arbuthnot Museum).

the rocket cart was within half a mile of the stranded vessel it bogged down on the sandy track and in order to save time the station officer went ahead with the rocket machine, rockets and line boxes. In spite of hitting the vessel, which turned out to be the steam trawler *Nairn*, with the first rocket, three further attempts failed. By this time District Officer Smailes had arrived from Peterhead and took charge of rescue operations. He had the rocket machine moved to a ledge below the cliff top and the rocket passed over the trawler. In spite of this the line parted as the whip was being hauled out when it fouled on rocks. Using spare line boxes as a rough platform for the machine the sixth rocket successfully landed a line aboard. While the hawser was being hauled out by the trawler's crew it fouled and was only kept clear by members of the life saving company climbing out over the rocks where they were at great risk of being swept away and drowned. Eventually the block was hauled out and secured but the whip again fouled while being hauled taut and was only freed through the heroic efforts of the Divisional Officer and three volunteers. Once the first man had been brought ashore the hawser had to be re-positioned before the remaining crew could be taken off as there was obviously considerable danger of the man in the buoy being dashed against intervening rocks by the heavy swell. The Collieston Lifesaving Company was awarded the Board of Trade Shield for the best wreck service in 1931. In addition the King awarded the Bronze Medal for Gallantry to Divisional Officer Smailes, Coastguard F. Shelley of Collieston and to Thomas Walker, John Henderson and John Walker of the Collieston Life Saving Apparatus.

Fog continued to be a major cause of shipping casualties in the pre-radar years of the 1930s when masters still had to shape their courses through a combination of experience, dead reckoning and luck in times of poor visibility. During 1933 the Aberdeen fishing fleet experienced severe casualties with three vessels lost at the beginning of the year on the north-east coast. In the case of the *Ben Screel* which stranded on Girdle Ness while returning from the fishing grounds the crew were only saved with great difficulty. She had arrived off Aberdeen in very thick fog which had partially blanketed the sound of the foghorn causing the trawler's skipper to steer too far south. A worker at the nearby sewer siphon house raised the alarm and by the time

16 The Aberdeen trawler *Ben Screel* hard aground on Girdle Ness after stranding in thick fog on 18 January 1933. (Aberdeen City Arts Department, Libraries).

the Torry rocket brigade arrived the *Ben Screel* was lying broadside to the shore and being swept by heavy seas. The seas made it impossible for her crew, who by now had taken refuge in the fore-mast and rigging, to retrieve the first line when it fell across the stern. They were more fortunate when the second engineer managed to secure the next line to the mast but the breeches buoy fouled while it was being pulled out to the trawler. Despairing of reaching the shore the second engineer pulled himself hand over hand along the hawser till he fell into the arms of the rescue party. In the gathering darkness a fire engine was called out, surely one of the few times that one has been summoned to a wreck, and two powerful searchlights were used to illuminate the wreck and shore. Finally with the breeches buoy back in action the remaining crewmen, by now suffering badly from the effects of wet and cold, were pulled ashore.

On 23 October of the same year in blinding rain and mist the Norwegian steamer *Granero* struck on Crawton Ness about three miles south of Stonehaven. She was spotted on the rocks shortly after dark by a local farmer, fully lit but making no distress signals. The Stonehaven rocket brigade arrived on the scene about two hours later but were hampered by lack of illumination until a searchlight was brought up. By three o'clock the following morning eleven men had been taken off with the master and six others electing to remain aboard. Due to the state of the tide neither of the lifeboats from Stonehaven could be launched and both the Aberdeen and Montrose lifeboats were called out with former standing by the casualty all night. Later that morning the Aberdeen lifeboat, *Emma Constance*, at the request of the master took off five more men and the ship's dog and landed them at Stonehaven. By early afternoon the steamer had broken her back and the master and chief engineer, having been persuaded not to abandon ship in a small dinghy, were taken on board the lifeboat.

In the latter 1930s a series of vessels stranded on the Caithness coast all of them in bad visibility. The Finnish steamer *Osterhav*, 4,293 tons gross ran ashore below the cliffs just south of Duncansby Head in dense fog on the evening of 28 March 1936. She had been bound for Finland to Ellesmere Port with a cargo of wood pulp. In spite of being badly holed she was able to refloat herself and head south for Wick. The Wick lifeboat was

17 Stonehaven LSA attending the stranded Norwegian steamer *Granero* after she went ashore at Crawton Ness south of Stonehaven in poor visibility on 23 October 1933. (Aberdeen City Arts Department, Art Gallery and Libraries).

launched and met the steamer off Freswick Bay to put aboard two pilots but with the water gaining on the pumps and nine feet of water in the forepeak she had to be run ashore at Reiss in Sinclair's Bay. After an extremely cold night standing by the casualty the lifeboat took off most of the steamer's crew and the ship's dog the following morning and landed them at Ackergill. While they were being embarked Captain Kartola ordered a bucket of tea to be passed over the side for the lifeboatmen. Later that afternoon with conditions steadily worsening the master and seven remaining members of the crew were taken off and landed at Wick by the lifeboat. At first there was little hope of refloating the *Osterhav* but the cargo of woodpulp swelled sufficently to allow the steamer to be refloated and beached at Cromarty for scrapping.

It is difficult now to appreciate the great hardships endured in bad weather by pre-war lifeboatmen. With little in the way of protection or shelter and the most basic of navigational aids they undertook rescue services without hesitation in conditions which were at times beyond belief. Consider, for example, the rescue of the crew of the King's Lynn collier *Fairy* by the Aberdeen lifeboat *Emma Constance* on 25 January 1937. Having arrived off Aberdeen after an appalling passage from Goole she had to lie off in a full south- east gale with very heavy seas and snow as the port was closed. As she tried to ride out the gale she started to take in water, some of it even coming down her tall funnel, and her master set the crew to bailing. With the stokehold knee-deep in water it proved impossible to maintain steam and there was little choice but to hoist distress signals. They were seen by the German trawler *Hendrick* whose crew managed to pass a hawser to the collier and take her in tow. In spite of this both vessels were gradually driven towards the land and by dusk they were off the mouth of the Don. A distress flare brought the call out of both Aberdeen lifeboats and two life-saving teams. In the huge seas running in the navigation channel the *Emma Constance* sustained considerable damage but was able to proceed northwards to where the two vessels were wallowing off the coast. At this point a nearby Swedish steamer signalled that she had problems with her steering gear and the lifeboat stood by her until there was no danger of her fouling the tow. In fact the hawser parted soon afterwards and it proved impossible to renew the tow in the atrocious weather which included heavy snow showers. The collier finally struck the beach at Millden Links north of Blackdog Rock and *Emma Constance* then ran in to take off the seven crew members. One huge sea threw her over the steamer's rail before another washed her back and her crew managed to leap aboard. As the lifeboat had no wireless she asked the Swedish steamer, which was still in the vicinity to signal to Aberdeen that the *Fairy*'s crew were safe. Given the terrible pounding that the lifeboat had experienced while leaving the harbour Coxswain Sinclair, by now unable to pass further signals, decided to run for shelter in the Moray Firth reaching Macduff at half past four the following morning. In the meantime there was acute anxiety back at Aberdeen when she failed to return to port which was only allayed when word was received of her safe arrival at Macduff. Coxswain Tom Sinclair was awarded a Silver Medal by the R.N.L.I. for this exceptionally arduous and dangerous rescue.

In April of the same year the Caithness coast south of Wick was the scene of another shipwreck when the 1157 ton Bergen steamer *Rein* ran ashore on Helman Head in thick weather early one Saturday morning. She had been steaming north for the Pentland Firth with a cargo of wood pulp for Preston, when without warning and too late to take any avoiding action, cliffs were sighted dead ahead and she ran on the rocks at full speed. Although distress flares were lit they could not be seen on shore as the steamer was lying close under the cliffs. The masthead light exploded with the force of the impact and the blaze was seen by Skipper Alexander Adamson of the local seine boat *Smiling Morn* which was on her way to the fishing grounds. As there were rocks on either side of the steamer which made it impossible to get alongside Skipper Adamson anchored off while the crew of the *Rein* launched their two lifeboats. In the heavy swell there was a considerable risk that the boats might be smashed against the stranded steamer and the last man to leave had to be picked up after jumping into the sea. At first light the crew reboarded their ship to try and save some personal effects but the receding tide made the attempt increasingly hazardous. They were landed at Wick and by the following high tide the steamer was completely awash.

With the Second World War only hours away the Wick

lifeboat, *City of Edinburgh* was called out shortly before midnight on 2 September 1939 to go to the aid of the Grimsby trawler *Navarre* ashore on Skirza Head. The lifeboat had already been on service earlier that day to escort the *Washington*, another Grimsby trawler, back to Wick after she had grounded in dense fog just north-east of Duncansby Head. Visibility remained poor and the trawler was eventually located in an extremely exposed position at the bottom of high flagstone cliffs. Two other trawlers were also standing by after an unsuccessful attempt to tow her off. As there was a considerable danger of the *Navarre* breaking up in the swell her skipper gave the order to abandon ship but the small boat was swept away and smashed on rocks. In pitch darkness, thick fog and heavy seas Coxswain Thain of the Wick lifeboat then ran alongside the trawler and took off nine men. Two others were saved by the local life-saving company using a line fired ashore earlier from the trawler.

Due to severe censorship restrictions reports of shipping casualties during the Second World War are superficial and very incomplete. Some fifty merchant vessels appear to have been sunk by enemy action in the immediate vicinity of the north-east coast with casualties concentrated off Rattray Head and the eastern approaches to the Moray Firth. The 4,666 ton Newcastle steamer *Cairnmona* bound from Canada with a cargo of wheat and copper was the first to be lost when she was torpedoed and sunk by the *U 13* on 30 October 1939 three miles off Rattray Head. She was the last ship in a small south bound convoy and lookouts at the nearby Coastguard Station saw her enveloped in a large explosion a few minutes before eleven o'clock at night. Within a quarter of an hour the Peterhead lifeboat had been launched and she picked up the forty-two survivors with three of the engine room staff and the ship's cat being lost. In 1973 a propeller and part of the copper were salvaged from the wreck which by this time had broken up.

With all coastal lights extinguished there were inevitably a number of instances of ships running ashore on the darkened coast. On the night of 11 December 1939 a vessel was sighted by Stonehaven Coastguards steering south-west and heading straight for Garron Point. They signalled her to stand out to sea but a few minutes later she ran on the rocks of Downie's Point just south of the harbour and immediately fired rockets and sounded her siren in distress signals. The life-saving apparatus were soon on the scene but the first line fired aboard parted almost immediately. A second was secured to a derrick by her crew but in the event it was not required as a ship's boat was used to ferry everyone ashore. The stranded steamer proved to be the *Cimbria* of Copenhagen bound in ballast for an east coast port. Having just missed striking dangerous rocks by a few yards she was relatively undamaged and refloated shortly afterwards.

There was heavy loss of life when the minesweeper, HMS *Sphinx*, was bombed fifteen miles north of Kinnairds Head on 2 February 1940 and sank the following day. From heavily censored newspaper reports it appears that she had been struck forward with her bow being bent upwards by the force of the blast. The engines had been put out of action and fuel oil was pumped over the side in what proved to be a disastrous attempt to calm the sea. One of the escorting vessels managed to pass a tow rope but this parted early the following day in the heavy swell. It proved impossible to keep the minesweeper's bow to the wind and she finally capsized. Those who were able to keep afloat became covered in oil with many choking to death before they could be saved. A final count revealed that fifty-four of her complement including the commanding officer had died. Bodies from her crew were washed ashore as far apart as Walls in Orkney and Wick.

Later that month and shortly before one o'clock in the morning of 14 February the watchkeeper at Wick Coastguard Station saw a violent explosion aboard a large ship steaming southwards. This proved to be the British tanker *Gretafield* with a cargo of fuel oil for Invergordon which had been struck by a torpedo from the *U 57*. Both Wick and Fraserburgh lifeboats were launched and twenty-seven survivors landed at Wick with fourteen of the tankers' crew reported missing believed killed. The tanker remained afloat and burning furiously finally drifted ashore at Dunbeath where she broke up the following month. For years after the war the rocky coasts of the Moray Firth carried a tide-line of tar as a reminder of the disaster.

In spite of the losses suffered by merchant shipping they could on occasion fight back and inflict casualties on the enemy. In the case of the 'North of Scotland' steamer *Highlander* which shot down two German aircraft in the summer of 1940 this had a fatal sequel. With practically nothing in the way of good news on the 'Home Front' at that time both press and radio unwisely gave the incident heavy coverage. From then on she appears to have been a marked ship and was renamed *St Catherine II* in an attempt to disguise her identity. After surviving several air attacks she was finally sunk off Aberdeen by an aerial torpedo on the evening of 14 November 1940 having just sailed from the port to join a north bound convoy. Captain J. G. Norquay, an extremely well liked master, thirteen of the crew and one passenger were drowned with seventeen survivors being picked up by the steamer *Berridale*.

For all the losses incurred by enemy action the weather proved in the end to be the most dangerous adversary. In January 1942 the British Isles were struck by a terrible hurricane accompanied by blinding snow-storms which led to major losses at sea. For the coxswain and crew of the Peterhead lifeboat it was to lead to the longest and most difficult services ever undertaken by one of the Institutions boats. The drama began before daylight on 23 January when the motor lifeboat *Julia Park Barry of Glasgow* escorted the Whitby registered steamers *Runswick* and *Saltwick* which had collided off Peterhead into the South Bay. They were also accompanied by the Glen Line steamer *Fidra* which was sheltering from the worsening weather. With the three vessels anchored in an extremely exposed position and in some danger of dragging ashore in the freshening wind the lifeboat remained on standby. Shortly after midnight she was called out when the *Runswick* fired distress flares as she started to drag towards the shore. By then the wind was blowing a full gale from the south-south-east with thick snow. Visibility having been reduced to virtually nil Coxswain John McLean was obliged to steer as best he could in the general direction of the steamer (which by now had taken the ground), until she switched on her searchlight. The Coxswain had great difficulty in remaining alongside the casualty due to the huge swell and eventually secured the lifeboat with four mooring ropes aft and one forward, the engine being run full astern to relieve the strain on the ropes. All forty-four of the steamer's crew were taken off, having to jump aboard from a pilot ladder, and were landed at the harbour.

After snatching a few hours sleep Coxswain McLean was back on watch later that morning along with the Second Coxswain and Mechanic and remained on standby for most of that day. By the morning of 25 January the wind had risen to hurricane force and at ten o'clock the *Saltwick* dragged ashore on the beach below the Lifeboat Secretary's house. The Life-Saving Apparatus fired a line aboard but this fouled and could not be freed. As the vessel was in no danger the crew were told to remain aboard but for unexplained reasons a boat manned by naval personnel rowed out and took off four men. This encouraged six of the crew to launch a raft but after an hour of being flung about by the surf two of the men were dead by the time they were dragged ashore. The remaining four were looked after by the lifeboat's Honorary Secretary.

At four o'clock that afternoon the *Fidra* finally went ashore in the continuing hurricane. When she sounded her siren in distress later that evening, the Life-Saving Company, still trying to free their gear at the *Saltwick*, went to her assistance. In spite of valiant efforts they were unable to establish contact and by midnight were collapsing from exhaustion. In answer to an urgent message for assistance from the *Fidra*'s master the lifeboat got under way at two o'clock in the morning (26 January) with the harbour's defence searchlight being switched on to provide illumination. In the huge seas Coxswain McLean had great difficulty in closing the stranded steamer and at one point was nearly swept aboard her by a particularly large wave. He finally moored alongside the steamer's boat-deck from where the crew managed to jump aboard, apart from one man with a sprained ankle who was dragged off by a lifeboatman. They finally returned to harbour with the leading lights lit to help guide them to safety.

The lifeboat's fourth and final service was undertaken shortly after daybreak to take off the men still aboard the *Saltwick* which by now was lying on her side with the seas breaking right over her. In order to try to get alongside in the lee of the ship the Coxswain had to try to sail between her and the shore. After striking the rocks several times and sustaining considerable damage to both the hull and deck fittings he managed to make fast on the sheltered side of the steamer's bow and take aboard thirty-six of the crew. The master and three officers elected to remain on board.

In all during the three days of the storm Coxswain McLean and the lifeboat's crew had undertaken four services and saved

106 lives. The Royal National Lifeboat Institution in recognition of the magnificent seamanship and heroism shown made the following awards: Coxswain John McLean, Gold Medal for conspicuous gallantry; Motor Mechanic David F. Wiseman, Silver Medal for gallantry; A. Hepburn, W. Summers, A. Gowans, A. Strachan, G. Cordiner and W. Strachan, Bronze Medal; A. Davidson the Institution's thanks on vellum. With Allied shipping suffering terrible losses due to the German submarine offensive, strenuous efforts were made to salvage the three steamers and by the following May they had been successfully refloated.

Apart from the casualties at Peterhead two other steamers were driven ashore on the Aberdeenshire coast during the storm, the *Empire Pilgrim* just north of Old Slains Castle in the early hours of 25 January and the Hull steamer *Lesrix* on Hackley Head shortly after midnight the following day. In the case of the former all of the crew were brought ashore by Collieston coastguards in an operation lasting three days. While they were fully occupied with this rescue flares were spotted off Hackley Head. At first there was some confusion as to the location and identity of the casualty with most telephone lines having been brought down in the continuing blizzard. As there were no other coastguard men at Collieston, Richard Ingram, a merchant officer home on leave and a local school boy George Ross, using spare gear managed to rescue four men by breeches buoy from the bow of the steamer which by this time had broken in two. The Newburgh lifeboat, John Ryburn, was also been called out but had to put back as she was unable to close the casualty which by then had been driven well up the rocks. Off the Ythan mouth she was caught on the beam by a huge breaking sea and capsized, trapping two men under the upturned hull. They managed to free themselves and all of the crew of seven were soon washed ashore. In spite of efforts by a rescue party which included two doctors, two of her crew died on the beach. To add to the tragedy the stern of the *Lesrix* broke away and sank with the loss of ten of her crew. Ingram was later awarded the Sea Gallantry Medal for the rescue while the unfortunate Ross, having failed to turn up for school that day, was rewarded with a severe rebuke for playing truant. Like the three casualties in Peterhead Bay every effort was made to salvage the *Empire*

Pilgrim and she was successfully refloated during the following month. The Newburgh lifeboat, having washed ashore on soft sand, suffered only superficial damage and remained at the station until it was closed in 1965.

It is difficult not to feel a little sorry for the unfortunate crew of the German submarine *U1206* which sank off Peterhead on 13 April 1945. She had sailed on her first and last patrol from Kristiansand on 6 April under the command of Kapitan Leutenant Adolf Schlitt with orders to patrol in the area of the Moray Firth. With the war obviously lost morale on board could not have been improved by the knowledge that in the immediate future the crew would be either dead or prisoners-of-war. Twenty-four hours after arriving on station the submarine developed a serious leak in the bow section which could not be controlled as the bilge pump failed. With his command about to sink Schlitt ordered the main ballast tanks to be blown and when the submarine surfaced the main diesel engines were started but promptly failed. All loaded torpedoes were fired to improve buoyancy, scuttling charges set and secret equipment destroyed. Although a brief report was sent to U-Boat Command the transmitter appears to have failed as well as it was never received. While the submarine was lying helplessly on the surface she was sighted by some minesweeping trawlers and challenged. Meanwhile the crew had abandoned ship in four rubber dinghies and cleared the submarine when the scuttling charges exploded. One of the Royal Navy trawlers had closed to engage and although she saw the *U1206* roll over and sink she failed to spot the Germans in the rafts. It was not until shortly before midnight that twenty-three men in two of the rafts were picked up by naval trawlers and landed at Aberdeen. Fourteen survivors on the third raft were rescued by a local fishing boat while the fourth containing ten survivors and one dead rating was washed ashore two miles south of Buchan Ness Lighthouse. Two other Germans were missing believed drowned.

11

Latter Days

With the coming of peace no vessel of substantial size was lost on the coast until the Sunderland collier *Marena* went ashore in a storm at Macduff on 28 February 1949 after breaking from her moorings. The majority of casualties were trawlers like the *Hassett* of Grimsby which grounded at the Ruff of Auckingill, Sinclair's Bay, in the early hours of 18 September 1953. She had been outward bound for the fishing grounds and struck in heavy seas. Both Wick Lifeboat and Life-Saving Apparatus had to search for several hours before the stranded trawler could be located. In that time five of the crew had been swept away and drowned while trying to clear the ship's boat. The destroyer HMS *Scorpion* had also answered the SOS but was forced to lie off with the lifeboat because of heavy breaking seas. Two lines were fired aboard from the shore but were out of reach of the crew who had gathered in the wheelhouse for safety. Communication was made at the third attempt using a line-throwing pistol and the fifteen survivors were all ashore by daybreak. One body was picked up by the lifeboat and three more recovered from the shore.

One of the most unhappy features of the Cold War was the total lack of trust between East and West. This was vividly illustrated when the Russian steamer *Krymov* bound for Aberdeen with a cargo of flax stranded off Murcar golf course north of the River Don on the night of 18 March 1956. Although both the Aberdeen Lifeboat and Bridge of Don life-saving crew were soon on the scene it proved impossible to make contact with anyone aboard, all signals being ignored. Worse still, when the life-saving crew managed to fire lines aboard, no attempt was made to secure them and in the end they gave up and returned to base. Similarly the lifeboat stood by for three hours while all her offers of help were ignored before returning to her station. The crew were in no immediate danger and stayed on the steamer for several days until an official from the Russian Embassy went aboard and persuaded them to abandon ship. She was eventually refloated and towed away for breaking up.

In spite of having been scuttled at Scapa Flow in 1919 salvage work on the German High Seas Fleet was still in progress forty years later although by then it was more of a tidying up operation. Certainly the author remembers the pier at Scapa in the 1950s piled high with cut up sections of gun barrels, armour plate and such like ready for shipping. Such cargoes are notoriously difficult to stow and are liable to shift in heavy weather. This is exactly what happened to the steamer *Sound Fisher* of Barrow shortly after sailing from Scapa with a cargo of scrap for Ghent on 13 January 1957. She had developed a list an hour after sailing which suddenly increased until the port rail was under water. Distress flares were fired and an SOS transmitted which alerted the Aberdeen trawlers *Woodbine* and *Dulcibelle* fishing nearby. It was well before daybreak when the master, Captain William Manderson, ordered the crew to abandon ship and the port lifeboat was launched in a choppy sea. This was crushed between the ship's side and the *Woodbine* and when the captain climbed in to try to free the boat it was swept away containing seven men. They were soon picked up none the worse by the *Dulcibelle* and landed at Aberdeen. In the meantime the *Woodbine* had rigged a breeches buoy to the stern of the *Sound Fisher* and taken off six men with the seventh jumping onto the trawler's bow. The steamer finally sank five hours after being abandoned four miles east-south-east of Wick.

The year 1959 was an especially tragic one for Caithness with the loss of no less than four ships between Duncansby Head and Dunbeath. On the morning of 9 January a workman at Thrumster reported that he had seen a vessel on fire at sea and shortly afterwards red flares were seen by the coastguards five or six miles off Wick. More flares were reported being burned off the coast by the keepers at Clyth Ness Lighthouse and a bus driver. Shortly before half past nine the British trawler *Summerlee* informed Wick radio that sixteen men had been picked up from a rubber dinghy by the Belgian trawler *St Jan Berchmans*. They were survivors from the fishery cruiser *Freya* which had foundered in rough seas a mile and a half east of Sarclet Head. Three of the crew including the master were missing but in spite of a search by the Wick lifeboat, the Life-Saving Apparatus and a naval helicopter there was no trace of them. The survivors reported that the Freya had been thrown on her beam-ends and then capsized with no chance of any distress messages being sent.

Almost exactly two months later the Swedish steamer *Stellatus*, with a cargo of wood pulp for Ellesmere Port, ran ashore in patchy fog on rocks just south of Buchollie Castle in the early hours of 3 March. By the time the Wick lifeboat and Life-Saving Apparatus arrived the steamer was lying parallel to the shore and listing slightly to starboard. Contact was established with the second rocket and the breeches buoy hauled out, but the first batch of men were in fact taken off by the lifeboat at midday. She then returned to the steamer which had lost all power due to the engine room flooding, and stood by till early evening when the captain abandoned ship with the remaining crew. A week later the steamer broke in two abaft the bridge during a south-east gale and the stern section sank, nearby beaches being strewn with wreckage.

Late on the night of 6 December with hurricane force winds blowing south-east Wick Radio intercepted a message from the Aberdeen trawler *George Robb* saying that she was ashore in the vicinity of Duncansby Head and asking for immediate assistance. Due to the sea state Wick lifeboat could not be launched and the crew of Life-Saving Apparatus had to search the coast on foot with the hurricane force winds throwing up huge sheets of spray and large sods of grass. In fact the wind was so strong that it was difficult to breath. Lights were sighted at the Stacks of Duncansby but by this time radio contact with the trawler had been lost. She was located by a searchlight lying on her port side completely submerged by heavy seas and no sign of life aboard. As there was no way that any assistance could be rendered the Life-saving crew withdrew to the shelter of Duncansby Head Lighthouse to renew their search at day break. In all twelve men were lost with only two bodies being washed ashore. To deepen the tragedy Station Officer Eric

18 The Swedish steamer *Stellatus* ashore near Buchollie Castle, Caithness, after stranding in thick fog on 3 March 1959. (Sutherland Manson, Thurso).

Campbell of Wick Coastguards collapsed and died on the cliffs while directing operations.

The same night the storm also disabled the 360 ton Leith registered motorship *Servas* off Lossiemouth when her propeller shaft broke. She was taken in tow by the fishery research vessel *Scotia* but the hawser had parted in the hurricane force winds and it proved impossible to pass another line aboard. With several vessels standing by, she was off the Caithness coast by midnight and both the Cromarty and Buckie Lifeboats were called out. At one point the vessel was struck by a massive wave which spun the ship's wheel so violently that the Second Engineer who was holding it was flung over in a complete somersault and badly bruised. The eight man crew, otherwise uninjured, were taken off by the Cromarty Lifeboat shortly before the *Servas* drifted ashore below Dunbeath Castle at two o'clock in the morning.

In the following decade there were remarkably few casualties and it was not until 1970 that disaster struck again. On the morning of 21 January the Fraserburgh Lifeboat, *Duchess of Kent*, went to the assistance of the Danish shrimp boat *Opal* which was labouring in heavy weather. While manoeuvring to come alongside she was flung upside down by a huge wave. One man, John Buchan the second mechanic, was thrown clear and picked up by the Russian mother-ship *Victor Kingisepp* whose crew frantically tried to right the capsized lifeboat. In the end the bodies of four of her crew trapped inside the hull were recovered with one man being unaccounted for. This had been the third Fraserburgh Lifeboat to be involved in a disaster, eight men having been lost in 1919 and six in 1953.

There was another unfortunate incident involving an Eastern Bloc vessel when the Polish trawler *Nurzec* ran ashore at Murcar, north of Donmouth, on the evening of 4 January 1974. She had been steaming off Aberdeen in gale force southerly winds waiting to enter the port and had been allowed to fall off too far to leeward. North of the River Don the bottom shelves gradually and the trawler had run on a sandbank some 400 yards offshore. The emergency services first learned of the incident when the police were phoned from Murcar Golf Club to say that two Polish seamen had just sought refuge at the club house. It transpired that the two men had abandoned ship in a liferaft which capsized in the surf and they had by some miracle reached the shore alive.

While the rescue services were being called out a Russian tug had arrived off Murcar and in a laudable but quite irresponsible rescue attempt had launched a lifeboat. In an outstanding feat of seamanship they managed to take off some of the crew from the *Nurzec* before their boat was overwhelmed in the surf and everyone thrown into the water. Nine survivors found shelter at Murcar club house, five men discovered on the beach were rushed to hospital and four bodies recovered from the upturned lifeboat. A British Airways S-61N scrambled from Dyce discovered another survivor on the beach further north. By this time the Aberdeen lifeboat had arrived offshore but was unable to find out what was going on as the Russian tug failed to answer any signals. As the water was too shallow to go alongside she lay off several hours before returning to port. The rescue services ashore, having accounted for all the survivors, fired a line over the trawler but this was not secured and in the end the eight men were winched off by helicopter the following morning. In all four men had lost their lives needlessly when, with a little cooperation everyone on the trawler could have been landed safely.

Two years later in an almost exact replica of the incident the Aberdeen trawler *Ben Gulvain* outward bound for the fishing grounds broke down shortly after leaving harbour. Repeated attempts by one of the harbour tugs to pass a hawser aboard failed and she drifted ashore on the beach just north of the Don. Conditions were bad with gale force winds raising heavy seas on the beach and the crew, who had launched two liferafts, remained on board after being advised to stay where they were by the lifeboat crew. Attempts to fire a line over the *Ben Gulvain* failed due to the strength of the wind and with the Lifeboat unable to close the casualty bacause of lack of water a British Airways rescue helicopter was called out. In a text book operation the crew of seventeen were winched off and landed on the golf course car park.

By the 1980s shipping casualties had dropped to an average of less than one per year a far cry from the terrible losses of the previous century. In fact the last notable wreck was on the evening of 19 December 1980 when the oil stand-by vessel *Ross Khartoum* suffered an engine failure shortly after leaving port

19 British Airways helicopter G-ATBY airlifts the crew of the Aberdeen trawler *Ben Gulvain* to safety after she had drifted ashore just north of Donmouth when her engines failed on 28 January 1976. (Isabella Deans, Aberdeen).

and drifted ashore on Balmedie beach. A harbour tug had made a vain attempt to take the converted trawler in tow but the tow ropes kept parting in the gale force winds and heavy swell. By the time the Aberdeen lifeboat arrived the ship was being swept from end to end by the swell but she could not get alongside because of the shallow water. Aboard the *Ross Khartoum* the eight man crew were in no danger and it was only when she started to drive northwards along the beach that the coastguards decided that they should be taken off. As Aberdeen Airport was closed by this time a Sea King rescue helicopter from RAF Lossiemouth was used to lift them to safety. The stand-by ship was driven so far up the beach that there was no chance of her being refloated and she was later cut up for scrap.

Appendix 1

Vessels Lost During Storm of 15–28 October 1875

Name	Date & Time	Location	Circumstances of Loss
Johann Cornelius	15 October, ?early a.m.	Off Ward of Cruden.	Brig of Rostock, broke adrift off Shields. Captain sole survivor.
Auguste	19 October, about 10 p.m.	1 mile south of Buchan Ness.	Schooner of Stettin, Norway for Thurso with timber. One man lost.
Julie Gaso	20 October, evening	Off Salthouse Head, Peterhead.	Schooner, identity uncertain. Foundered with loss of crew.
John Murray	21 October, 10.30 a.m.	Burnmouth Rock, Muchalls.	Schooner of Exeter, disabled and drove ashore. Crew lost.
Dorothy Jobson	21 October, c. 4.30 p.m.	Off Stonehaven	Brig of Blyth, sank with loss of 8 men.
John & Isabella Smith	21 October, 10.00 p.m.	Dunnottar, south of Stonehaven.	Brig of Shields, drove ashore and lost with all hands.
Superior	22 October, 1.30 a.m.	1 mile south of Muchalls.	Brig of Kalmar. Hull for Copenhagen coal-laden. Wrecked, 8 lost.
Hjack	22 October, 4.00 a.m.	2 miles north of Scotstown Head.	Barque of Langesund. Coal-laden for Norway, Crew saved by LSA.
Isabella Miller	22 October, 11.00 a.m.	1 mile north of Aberdeen.	Schooner of Colchester. In ballast for H'pool, crew saved by lifeboat
Baumeister Kraeft	22 October, c. 2.00 p.m.	Near Peterhead harbour.	Prussian schooner. For Newcastle timber-laden 3 lost saving crew.

Nathalia Jacobsina	22 October, c. 6.00 p.m.	South Harbour, Peterhead.	Danish sloop, driven ashore. Crew saved. Later refloated.
Behrend	22 October, c. 8.00 p.m.	Waterhaven, south of Boddam.	Barque of Memel, drove ashore derelict. Crew lost. Timber laden.
Olga	22/23 October	Forvie Sands, north of River Ythan	Finnish brigantine, Coal-laden for C'hagen Crew saved by LSA.
Mediateur	23 October, 5.00 a.m.	Boar's Head, Spey Bay.	French schooner, in ballast, crew saved by LSA. Possibly salvaged
Minnie	28 October	Whinnyfold, Cruden Bay.	Brig of Sandby. Driven ashore derelict.

Appendix 2

Vessels Lost During Storm of 22–23 December 1876

Name	Date & Time	Location	Circumstances of Loss
Anna	?22 December.	Between Golspie and Little Ferry.	Schooner? Driven ashore, no survivors.
Johanna	22 December, daybreak.	Garron Point, Stonehaven.	Barque of Danzig, for London. Broke up with loss of 13 and 1? woman.
William	22 December, post 9.30 a.m.	Eigie, Balmedie Links, north of River Don.	Brig of Mandal. Driven ashore with loss of crew, ship's dog only survivor
Alida	22 December, post 11.00 a.m.	Off Rattray Head.	?Prussian barque. Sank with loss of all hands.
Foldin	22 December, 1.00 p.m.	Stonehaven, back of Old Pier.	Barque of Sandefjord. Driven ashore derelict. Crew lost.
Christine	22 December, 2.30 p.m.	North of Donmouth.	Brig of Horten. Drove ashore and broke up with loss of crew of 9.
Louise Elizabeth	22 December, post 2.30 p.m.	Off Blackdog north of Donmouth.	Barque of Holmstrand. Foundered with loss of all hands.
Christian Marie?	*22 December, ?4.00 p.m.*	*Skateraw, north of Donmouth.*	*German galliot. Lost with all hands.*
* A	22 December, 5.00 p.m.	North of Cove.	Brig? Unidentified, lost with all hands.
Karen Nickelsten? *	22 December, between 5.00 –11.00 p.m.	Between Cove and Aberdeen.	Identity uncertain. Lost with all hands. Stern board washed ashore.

Au Revoir	22 December, 6.00 p.m.	Keiss Castle, Caithness.	Russian barque. Havre for Riga. Crew saved.
Courier	22 December, 7.00 p.m.	Craig Garmaig Rock, Dornoch.	Brig of Barth. From Hull coal-laden. Wrecked with only one survivor.
Johanna	22 December, 7.00 p.m.	Cowie Beach, Stonehaven.	Brig of Norway. Driven ashore, crew saved by LSA.
B	22 December, post 7.00 p.m.	Vicinity Old Cowie Churchyard.	Unidentified. Driven ashore with loss of crew.
C	22 December, c. 11.00 p.m.	North of Cove.	Unidentified. Driven ashore with loss of crew.
Maas Affrighter	22 December, late p.m.?	Off Tain.	Schooner? Driven ashore, crew lost.
Frederick II	22/23 December	Near Findon Ness north of Stonehaven.	German? Driven ashore, no survivors. Identity uncertain.
Marie Julie	22/23 December	Swiney near Lybster.	Brig of Memel. Wrecked with loss of 8 men.
D	22/23 December	May Crags, Muchalls.	Unidentified. Driven ashore, no survivors.
Adler	23 December, a.m.	Tain Bar.	German schooner. For the Forth timber-laden, crew saved.
Vidar	23 December, post 1.00 a.m.	Drum's Burn south of Ythanmouth.	Norwegian brig. Granton for Arendal with coal. Crew saved.
Vesta	23 December, 2.00 a.m.	Between Embo and Coull.	Russian barque. Granton for Kiel. Driven ashore, crew saved.
Enighed	23 December, 4.00 a.m.	Balmedie Links, north of River Don.	Norwegian brig. Coal-laden for Norway, 1 man lost.
Sophie	23 December, 5.00-6.00 a.m.	Near Salthouse Head, Peterhead Bay.	Norwegian brig. Drifted ashore derelict, crew lost.
Allardic	23 December, pre-8.00 a.m.	Onnichie, Rattray Head.	Norwegian barque. Run ashore by master. Crew saved in ship's boat.

Emelie	23 December, c. 8.00 a.m.	Ackergill, Sinclair Bay.	German schooner. For Wolgast with coal. 5 crew and 3 rescuers lost
Pallamatta	23 December, 10.00 a.m.	Scaurs of Cruden.	Unidentified barque. Driven ashore with loss of crew of ?12.
Tijsiena	23 December, ?11.00 a.m.	Charleston, St Combs.	Dutch galliot. Bergen for Holland with dried fish. Crew saved.
Angela	23 December, 11.00 a.m.	Strathbeg Bay, north of Rattray Head.	Brig of and for Dramm with iron from Grimsby. Crew saved by LSA.
Alexander	23 December, c. 3.30 p.m.	Stotfield Skerries, Lossiemouth.	Barque of Danzig. Drove ashore with loss of crew.
Johanne	23 December, post 3.30 p.m.	North of Donmouth.	Danish brig. Coal-laden for Aarhus, crew washed ashore on deckhouse.

* May be same casualty.

Appendix 3

Vessels Lost During Storm of 4–6 March 1881

Name	Date & Time	Location	Circumstances of Loss
Mars	?4 March	Entrance to Aberdeen Harbour.	Brig of and for Aberdeen coal-laden.
Flower of Buchan	5 March, 4.00 p.m.	Below Ackergill L/B. Shed, Sinclair's Bay.	Schooner, Peterhead for Sunderland in ballast. Crew saved.
Sprightly	?5 March	Off Aberdeen?	Brig of Folkestone. Wreck washed ashore. Crew lost.
Concordia	?5 March	Freswick Bay.	Schooner of Mandal. Washed ashore capsized and derlict. Crew lost.
John Hannah	?5 March	Off Peterhead?	Brigantine of Ramsgate Wreckage washed ashore. Crew lost.
Havelock	5/6 March	Garron Point, Stonehaven.	Schooner of Colchester Driven ashore with loss of crew.
Maldon	6 March, 6.30 a.m.	Cruden Sands, Port Erroll.	Schooner of and from Maldon for Newcastle. Crew saved by LSA.
Friedrich Perthes	6 March, 9.00 a.m.	Inverallochy	Barque of Bremen. USA–Granton. 1 man lost.
Ben Rhydding	6 March, 9.00– 10.00 a.m.	Blackdog, north of Donmouth.	Full rigged ship of Liverpool. Calcutta to Dundee with jute. Crew of 28 lost.

Why Not	6 March, 10.00 a.m.	The Skerry, Peterhead.	Brig of Bridport. Forth for France with coal. Lost with all hands.
Ann Williams	6 March, post 10.30 a.m.	Vicinity of Blackdog.	Schooner of Padstow. 6 lost, only 1 survivor.
Royal Eagle	6 March, 11.00 a.m.	Cruden Sands, Port Erroll.	Schooner of London. For Sunderland with pipe-clay. Crew saved by LSA.
Helen	6 March, ?11.00 a.m.	Menie Links, north of Donmouth.	Schooner of Faversham. London–Tyne in ballast. Crew saved.
Josef	6 March, ?11.00 a.m.	2 miles south of Ythanmouth.	Brig of Friesburg. Amsterdam to Aberdeen with bones. Crew lost.
Wanderer	6 March, 11.20 a.m.	To north of Blackdog.	Schooner of Southampton. For Jarrow with wood. Only one survivor.
Moreford & Trueby	6 March, 5.00p.m.	Donmouth.	Schooner of Chester. Newcastle-Ancona with coal. Crew saved by Aberdeen lifeboat.

Bibliography

The following unpublished sources have been consulted:

Aberdeen – City Archives: Propinquity Books, Volumes 1-3, Council In-Letters, 17th and 18th Century.

Coastguard Headquarters: Permanent Station Records – Aberdeen, Collieston, Fraserburgh, Peterhead, Rattray Head, Rosehearty and Stonehaven.

Edinburgh – Scottish Record Office: Registers of the Privy Council of Scotland, Seafield Muniments, Kinross House Papers, Gordon Castle Muniments, Register House Series - RH 15, Customs and Excise Outport Records, Aberdeen and Thurso, Sheriff Court Records – Aberdeen and Wick.

Kew – Public Record Office: Admiralty Files.

Poole – R.N.L.I. Headquarters: Station Records – Aberdeen, Cromarty, Buckie, Fraserburgh, Peterhead, Port Erroll and Stonehaven.

BOOKS

The sources listed below were the principal ones consulted:

Adams, I. H. and Fortune C., *Alexander Lindsay, A Rutter of the Scottish Seas*, (London, 1980).

Alison, J. (ed), *Poetry of Northeast Scotland*, (London, 1976).

Allardyce, K. and Hood E. M., *At Scotland's Edge*, (Edinburgh, 1986).

Anderson, P. F., *Robert Stewart, Earl of Orkney and Lord of Shetland*, (Edinburgh, 1982).

Brown, D., *Warship Losses of World War Two*, (London, 1990).

Clark, V. E., *The Port of Aberdeen*, (Aberdeen, 1921).

Close-Brooks, J., *The Highlands*, (London, 1986).

Collins, G., *Great Britain's Coasting Pilot*, (London, 1693).

Cranna, J., *Fraserburgh Past and Present*, (Aberdeen, 1914).

Cranna, J., *A Record of Shipwrecks in the Fraserburgh District*, Transactions of the Buchan Field Club, (Peterhead,1923).

Donaldson, G., *Northwards by Sea*, (Edinburgh, 1966).

Duthie, J. L., *To the Rescue*, (Aberdeen, 1981).

Farr, A. D., *Let Not the Deep*, (Aberdeen, 1973).

Gosset, W. P., *Lost Ships of the Royal Navy*, (London, 1986).

Groner, E., *Die deutschen Kriegsschiffe 1815–1945*, (Munich, 1966).

Hakluyt, R., *The Discovery of Muscovy*, (London, 1889).

Hampshire, A. C., *They Called It Accident*, (London, 1961).

Hocking, C. (ed), *Dictionary of Disasters at Sea during the age of Steam*, (London, 1969).

Jeffries, R. and McDonald, K., *The Wreck Detectives*, (London, 1969).

Mitchell, J., *Reminiscences of My Life in the Highlands*, (Newton Abbot, 1966).

Rohwer, J., *Axis Submarine Successes 1939–1945*, (Annapolis, 1971).

Ross, S., *Sail Ships of Orkney*, (Kirkwall, 1954).

Simpson, G. G., *Scottish Handwriting 1150–1650*, (Aberdeen, 1973).

Smith, H. D., *Shetland Life and Trade 1550–1914*, (Edinburgh, 1984).

Stern, W. M., *Britain Yesterday and Today*, (London, 1962).

Taylor, L. B.(ed), *Aberdeen Council Letters. Volume I, (1552–1633)*, (Oxford, 1942).

Taylor, L. B.(ed), *Aberdeen Council Letters. Volume III, (1645–1660)*, (Oxford, 1952).

Young, J. M., *Britain's Sea War*, (Wellingborough, 1989).

Zanelli, L., *Unknown Shipwrecks Around Britain*, (London, 1974).

GAZETEERS

Aberdeen Journal – Notes and Queries, (Aberdeen, 1888 and 1893).

British Vessels Lost at Sea 1914–1918 and 1939–1945, (Cambridge, 1988).

Biographical Dictionary of Living Naval Officers, (London?, 1849).

Conway's All the World's Fighting Ships 1860–1905, (London, 1978).

Conway's All the World's Fighting Ships 1906–1921, (London, 1985).

Dictionary of National Biography, (London, 1908).

Extracts From the Council Register of the Burgh of Aberdeen, 1398–1570, (Aberdeen, 1844).

Lloyds War Losses – The Second World War, Volume I, (London, 1989)

Merchant Shipping 1913–14: Return of Shipping Casualties and Loss of Life for the Year Ended 30 June 1914, Cmd 984, (London, 1920).

Merchant Shipping 1 July 1914–31 December 1918: Return of Shipping Casualties and Loss of Life for the Period Ended 31 December 1918, Cmd 1089, (London, 1921).

North Coast of Scotland Pilot, (Taunton, 1975).
North Sea (West) Pilot, (Taunton, 1973).
The Edinburgh Geographical and Historical Atlas, (Edinburgh, 1842?).

PERIODICALS

Aberdeen Daily Journal
Aberdeen Free Press
Aberdeen Herald
Aberdeen Journal
Aberdeen Weekly Journal
Banffshire Advertiser
Buchan Observer
Caithness Courier
Daily Free Press
Edinburgh Evening Courant
Elgin Courant
Forres Gazette
Fraserburgh Herald
Herald and Weekly
Free Press
Invergordon Times
Inverness Courier

Inverness Journal
John O' Groat Journal
Lloyds List
Lloyds Register of Shipping
Moray and Nairn Express
Moray Weekly News
Northern Ensign
Northern Scot
Orcadian
Orkney Herald
Press and Journal
Scottish Highlander
Shetland Life
Steel's Correct List of the Royal Navy
The Lifeboat
The Mariner's Almanac

Index of Ships Wrecked

(Note (s) indicates vessel salvaged)

Caledonia (s)	1895	Brig, Norwegian	80–2
Charsten & Peter	1815	Galliot, Danish	32
Chicago	1894	Steamer, British	78
Christiana	1803	Full-rigged ship, Norwegian	26
Christian Marie	1876	Galliot, German	65, 129
Christine	1876	Brig, Norwegian	129
Cimbria (s)	1939	Steamer, Danish	113
City of Osaka	1930	Steamer, British	102–4
Concordia	1881	?Schooner, Norwegian	132
Countess of Aberdeen	1894	Steamer, British	76–8
Courier	1876	Brig, German	130
Daniel Stroud			
HM Trawler	1915	Steam trawler, British	96
De Leeuw (s)	1856	Galliot, Dutch	49
Dorothy Jobson	1875	Brig, British	60, 127
Duchess of Kent	1970	Lifeboat, British	122
Duke of Richmond	1859	Paddle steamer, British	49–50
Duke of Sutherland	1853	Paddle steamer, British	45–8
Duncan	1716	'Galley', British	13–4
Dunstaffnage	1883	Full-rigged ship, British	71–2
Earl of Derby	1796	Unknown, British	21–2
Echo	1928	Steamer, Norwegian	100, 102
Edward Bonaventure	1556	Unknown, English	5–6
Elizabeth	1697	Unknown, British	10
Emelie	1876	Schooner, German	65–6, 131
Empire Pilgrim (s)	1942	Steamer, British	116–7
Enighed	1876	Brig, Norwegian	130
Erne HMS	1915	Destroyer, British	96
Fairy	1937	Steamer, British	110–1
Falcoun	1584	Unknown, Norwegian	6
Fame	1830	Smack, British	35–6
Fidra (s)	1942	Steamer, British	114–5
Flower of Buchan	1881	Schooner, British	70, 132
Foldin	1876	Barque, Norwegian	129
Fram	1940	Steamer, Swedish	x, xi
Frederick II	1876	Unknown, German?	130
Frederick Snowden	1912	Steamer, British	92, 93
Freya	1959	Fishery Cruiser, British	120
Friedrich Perthes	1881	Barque, German	132
Friendship	1786	Unknown, British	21
Fussroun Geertruy	1708	Dogger, Dutch	11
G103	1925	Destroyer, German	99
George Robb	1959	Motor trawler, British	120
Gerona (s)	1892	Steamer, British	74–6
G. Koch	1913	Steamer, Danish	93, 94
Goodenough	1809	Schooner, Danish	29
Grace Darling	1874	Barque, British	56–7

Martha & Mary	1760	Snow, British	19–20
Marthas	1822	Sloop, British	33
Mary	1803	Full-rigged ship, British	27
Mazinthien	1883	Steam whaler, British	72–4
Mediateur	1875	Schooner, French	63, 128
Minnie	1875	Brig, Norwegian	64, 128
Moreford & Trueby	1881	Schooner, British	133
Nairn	1931	Steam trawler, British	106
Nancy & Katty	1803	Full-rigged ship, Swedish	26
Nar	1904	Steamer, British	86
Natal HMS	1915	Armoured cruiser, British	97
Nathalia Jacobsina (s)	1875	Sloop, Danish	62, 127
Navarre	1939	Steam trawler, British	112
Neptune	1799	Unknown, British	23
Noordpool	1931	Steam trawler, Dutch	104–5
Norval (s)	1818	Brig, British	32–3
Nurzec	1974	Motor trawler, Polish	122–3
Ohio (s)	1897	Steamer, British	82
Olga	1875	Brigantine, Russian	63, 128
Olive	1849	Schooner, British	43–4
Oscar	1813	Whaler, British	30–2
Osterhav	1936	Steamer, Finnish	108, 110
Pallamatta	1876	Barque, Unknown	131
Pasha	1865	Barque, British	52
Peggy & Mary	1800	Sloop, British	24
Phaeton	1800	Brig, Swedish	24
Pitstruan HM Trawler	1917	Minesweeper, British	97
Primrose	1811	Brigantine, British	30
Prince Consort (s)	1863	Paddle steamer, British	51
Prince Consort	1867	Paddle steamer, British	53–4
Providence	1815	Schooner, British	32
Pylades (s) HMS	1811	Sloop of war, British	29–30
Rein	1937	Steamer, Norwegian	111
Reliance	1803	Unknown, British	25–6
Ross Khartoum	1980	Oil stand-by vessel, British	123, 125
Royal Eagle	1881	Schooner, British	133
Runswick (s)	1942	Steamer, British	114
St Catherine II (ex *Highlander*)	1940	Steamer, British	114
St Clair (s)	1895	Steamer, British	78–80
St Giles	1902	Steamer, British	85
St George	1874	Lifeboat, British	56
St Magnus	1918	Steamer, British	97–8
St Nicholas	1728	Unknown, Swedish	16–7
St Nicholas	1914	Steamer, British	93, 95
Saltwick (s)	1942	Steamer, British	114–5
Salvor No I	1915	Steamer, British	96

'Ane great fleboat'	1639–1648	Unknown, British	8
–	1677	Unknown, British	10
–	1703	Unknown, unknown	10–1
–	1800	Unknown, unknown	23
–	1800	Unknown, unknown	23
–	1800	Brig, British	23
–	1800	Brig, British	23
–	1800	Brig, unknown	23
–	1800	Sloop, unknown	23
–	1800	Sloop, unknown	23
A	1876	Brig?, unknown	129
B	1876	Unknown, unknown	130
C	1876	Unknown, unknown	130
D	1876	Unknown, unknown	130

General Index

Centre for Scottish Studies, University of Aberdeen, Old Aberdeen, AB9 2UB.
Telephone 0224–272474.
Director and Editor of Pamphlets: Dr John S Smith (Department of Geography)
Editor of Northern Scotland: Professor Peter L. Payne (Department of History)
Conference Organiser: Mr A. Rodney Gunson (Department of Geography)

NORTHERN SCOTLAND is the annual journal of the centre. Full details on subscription, content, availability of back numbers, from the Centre.

CENTRE PAMPHLETS (in print)
(Available from bookshops, the Queen Mother Library and the Centre)

Alexander Carlyle, *Journal of a tour to the North of Scotland (1765)*	£1.00
R.E.H. Mellor & J.S. Smith, *Visitors' Guide to Aberdeen*	£2.50
D.P. Willis, *Sand and silence. Lost villages of the North*	£3.00
John McLaren, *Sixty Years in an Aberdeen Granite Yard. The Craft* and the Men	£5.90
David Toulmin, *The Tillycorthie story*	£4.50
Roy Howard, *Cults, past and present*	£5.00
David Summers, *Fishing off the Knuckle. The Story of Buchan's fishing villages*	£3.00
Nancy H. Miller, *Peterhead and the Edinburgh Merchant Company. Visits by the Governors to their Buchan estates, 1728–1987.*	£3.00
James S. Wood, *For Heaven's Sake*	£3.00

PUBLISHED JOINTLY BY THE CENTRE AND INSTITUTE OF TERRESTRIAL ECOLOGY

Caring for the High Mountains. Conservation of the Cairngorms Edited by J.W.H. Conroy, Adam Watson and A.R. Gunson	£6.00

Prices include postage. Cheques should be made payable to the Centre for Scottish Studies.

PUBLICATIONS BY ABERDEEN UNIVERSITY PRESS SPONSORED BY THE CENTRE
(Available from bookshops and the Centre)

New Light on Medieval Aberdeen. Edited by John S. Smith	£4.95
Robert Barclay, *Reminiscences of an unlettered man.* Edited by David Stevenson	£4.95
From lairds to louns. Country and burgh life in Aberdeen, 1600–1800. Edited by David Stevenson	
Aberdeen in the nineteenth century. The making of a modern city. Edited by John S. Smith and David Stevenson	£4.95
Covenant, Charter and Party. Traditions of Revolt and Protest in Modern Scottish History. Edited by Terry Brotherstone	£9.95
Grampian Battlefields. The Historic Battles of North-East Scotland from AD40 to 1745. By Peter Marren	£9.95
From Aberdeen to Ottawa in 1845. The Diary of Alexander Muir. Edited by George A. MacKenzie	£5.95
North East Castles. Edited by John S. Smith	£5.95
Diary of a Canny Man. Edited with an introduction by David Stevenson	£6.95
Shipwrecks of North East Scotland 1444–1990 David M Ferguson	£6.95